MW01250720

CHRIST IS COMING; THE ANTICHRIST IS REVEALED

CHRIST IS COMING; THE ANTICHRIST IS REVEALED

BY:

Debra Barclay

I was on the cross
I was on the cross, and you took me down
You have trampled my blood
Lift me up
Lift me high for all to see
For vengeance is mine, saith the Lord.

Copyright © 1997, 2000 by Debra Barclay

All rights reserved. No part of this book may be reproduced,
stored in a retrieval system, or transmitted by any means,
electronic, mechanical, photocopying, recording, or otherwise,
without written permission from the author.

ISBN 1-58500-157-0

1st Books-rev. 3/31/00

HIS DEADLY WOUND WILL BE HEALED!
Nebuchadnezzar, *ruler* over *Babylon*,
"Thou art the *head* of gold."
Ruler = head - for head in the above means ruler according
to the Strong's Concordance.

Rev. 13, "(v. 1) And I stood upon the sand of the sea, and saw a beast rise up out of the sea, having seven heads [or 7 rulers] and ten horns . . . (v. 2) the dragon gave him his <u>power</u>, and his **_SEAT_**, and <u>great authority</u>. And I saw one [<u>or the "first," esp. in coming] of his heads</u> **_AS_** it were wounded to death [the "first" in coming who will take "priority" of the 7 leaders/heads will be *as* it were wounded to death. In other words, he doesn't die just his leadership/head. Also, what is John talking about in Rev. 13:2 . . . the beast's rule hence his seat! Netanyahu, the first in coming of the 7 leaders has temporarily lost his seat.] . . . **_and his deadly wound was healed_**."

Rev. 17:10 speaks of the *rise* and *fall* of kings. Verse 11 continues speaking of the Antichrist, "And the beast that was, and is not, even he is the eighth, and is of the seven, and goeth into perdition."

<u>At the time he was prophesied over to be the Antichrist, Benjamin Netanyahu was in office.</u>

Table of Contents

Introduction

Revelation chapter 10, tells of a little open book
that carries a message. This book's message has
remained sealed up until the appointed time.
This is that time and this is that book!
*"This is the light that shineth
in the darkness."*

Revelation chapter 10:

(v. 1) And I saw another mighty angel come down from
heaven, clothed with a cloud: and a rainbow was upon his
head, and his face was as it were the sun, and his feet as
pillars of fire: (v. 2) And he had in his hand a *little book
open* [before it was shut]: and he set his right foot upon
the sea, and his left foot on the earth [this message that the
little book carries will travel over land and sea], (v. 3) And
cried with a loud voice, as when a lion roareth: and when
he had cried, seven thunders uttered their voices [or the
mysteries of God]. (v. 4) And when the seven thunders
had uttered their voices, *I was about to write*: and I heard
a voice from heaven saying unto me, *Seal up* those things
which the seven thunders uttered, and *write them not* [*it
was not yet time to write the mysteries of God*]. (v. 5)
And the angel which I saw stand upon the sea and upon the
earth lifted up his hand to heaven, (v. 6) And *sware* by him
that liveth for ever and ever, who created *heaven*, and the
things that **therein** *are*, and the *earth*, and the things that
therein *are* [God made an unbreakable sacred promise of
projection concerning His message. God in His
foreknowledge knows everything; God projected by
heaven and earth that His message would come to pass.],
and the sea, and the things which are therein, that there
should be *time no longer*: (v. 7) But in the days of the
voice of the seventh angel, when he *"shall begin to sound"*

[in the fullness of time when the voice will have been heard], the mystery of God should be finished, as he hath declared to his servants the prophets.

The apostle Peter spoke in II Peter chapter 1:
(v. 16) we have not followed cunningly devised fables, when we made known unto you the ***power and coming of our Lord Jesus Christ, but were eyewitnesses of his majesty***. (v. 17) For he received from God the Father honour and glory, when there came such a voice to him from the *excellent glory* [because our walk is from glory to glory, II Cor. 3:16-18], This is my beloved Son, in whom I am well pleased. (v. 18) And this voice which came from heaven we heard, when we were with him in the ***holy mount***. (v. 19) We have ***also a more sure word of prophecy***; whereunto *ye do well that ye take heed*, as unto ***a light that shineth in a dark place***, until the day dawn, and the day star arise in your hearts.

Peter is declaring that there is *a more sure word of prophecy concerning the power and coming of our Lord Jesus Christ.* In this last day, people should expect to receive an updated version of a word of prophecy concerning the power and Second Coming of Christ. **These are the mysteries of God that have been** ***sealed up until it was time to write***. Peter connects this biblical perspective of a last day message, concerning the power and the coming of Christ in with what he and the other apostles saw on the holy mount. While on the *holy mount* a voice came to the apostles, and Matthew chapter 17 speaks of this day:
(v. 1) And ***after six days*** [the 6000th year into the future] Jesus taketh Peter, James, and John his brother, and bringeth them up into an high mountain apart, (v. 2) And was transfigured before them: and his face did shine as the sun, and his raiment was white as the light [it was a time for Christ to be more glorified]. (v. 3) And, behold, there appeared unto them Moses and Elias talking with him. [In this last day two witnesses are going to arise who have been talking with God gaining knowledge.] (v. 4) Then

answered Peter, and said unto Jesus, Lord, it is good for us to be here: if thou wilt, let us make here three tabernacles; one for thee, and one for Moses, and one for Elias. (v. 5) While he yet spake, behold, <u>a bright cloud overshadowed them</u>: and behold a voice out of the cloud, which said, *This is my beloved Son, in whom I am well pleased; hear ye him*.

This cloud which overshadowed Moses, Elias, and Christ symbolized that in this last day, the sixth day, Christ is going to talk to the people through two witnesses. Spoken of in Rev. ch. 11, these two witnesses will come in the spirit and power of Moses and Elias, or Elijah of the Old Testament. *Moses' presence with Christ on the mount on the sixth day represented a fulfillment of time*. Recall that when John the Baptist had baptized Jesus, this same voice as the three apostles had heard on the holy mount came from heaven to say, "This is my beloved Son in whom I am well pleased" (Matthew 3:17). Christ instructed us in Matthew 3:13-17 that He performed the baptism to "*fulfill all righteousness*." Christ did not come to destroy the *law but to fulfill it* (Matt. 5:17). Jesus came to fulfill the Old Testament Law that was perfect, but because mankind was imperfect, no one could live by it. Now, the OT Law that Christ came to fulfill, what was it? It was *Scripture* that Moses had written. This is the reason why, as the voice once again comes from heaven that Moses is present with Christ on the holy mount. God, in this last day, the sixth day, is going to come to *fulfill all Scripture!* Even some of the plagues delivered in Moses' day, Exodus 7-11, testify of this fact, for they are a foreshadowing of the plagues poured out at the end of time in Revelation chapter 16, the last book of God's Holy Scripture. Just as Revelation 10:7 suggests, "But in the days of the voice of the seventh angel, when he shall begin to sound [in the fullness of time when the voice will have been heard], the mystery of God should be finished, as he hath declared to his servants the prophets."

Elias' presence with Christ on the mount signified God's plan for the end of the ages. Elias, seen with Christ on the sixth day, represented another individual that shall not only come in the spirit and power of Elias, but this individual will perform the same divine purpose as John the Baptist. Matthew chapter 17 continues:

> (v. 9) And as they came down from the mountain [because this will be a mountain-top experience], Jesus charged them, saying, Tell the vision to no man, until the Son of man be *risen again from the dead*. [Jesus was saying I have **_NOT YET BEEN GLORIFIED_**, and still you saw Elias standing by me while *I was in a glorified body*.] (v. 10) And his disciples asked him, saying, Why then say the scribes that Elias must *first* come? [The apostles knew, according to what the prophets had written (Malachi 4:5) that Elias was supposed to appear *"before"* Christ was *glorified*. But Elias' presence standing by a glorified Christ on the mount signified that Elias would appear *"again"* in this last day, the sixth day, *before* the Second Coming.] (v. 11) [For] Jesus answered and said unto them, Elias truly *"shall"* [because He just showed them the 6000th yr. into the future] first come, and restore all things. [Christ then in this next verse ties in the name of that Elias with John the Baptist.] (v. 12) But I say unto you, That Elias is come already, and they knew him not, but have done unto him whatsoever they listed. Likewise shall also the Son of man suffer of them. (v. 13) Then the disciples understood that he spake unto them of John the Baptist.

In this biblical context, Elias represented a witness who will have a two-fold purpose in the plan of God. *First of all this witness, like John the Baptist, will have the office of one preparing the way for Christ's Second Coming*. Jesus spoke, "(Matt. 11:11) there hath not risen a greater than John the Baptist [it was John's message that was so great]: notwithstanding he that is least in the kingdom of heaven is greater than he . . . . (Matt. 11:13) For all the *__prophets__* and the *__law__* prophesied until John." Referring back then to the *__Old Testament prophet__* Isaiah, John was "The voice of him that crieth in the wilderness, Prepare ye the way of the LORD" (Isa. 40:3). Jesus then continued His statement in Matt. 11:14, "And if ye will receive it [what was just spoken of the OT prophet concerning John], *THIS is Elias*, which was for to come." In other words this Elias which was for to come and John the Baptist have only the *same office* in common. For John, after the lineage of a high priest because his mother was of the daughters of Aaron (Luke 1:5), knew whom he was when the people asked him, "(v. 21) What then? Art thou Elias? And he saith, **I AM NOT** . . . . (v. 23) [But John was] the *voice* of one crying in the wilderness, Make straight the way of the Lord" (John 1:21, 23).

Secondly this witness, unlike John the Baptist who never performed a miracle (John 10:41), will wrought miracles similar to that of Elijah. Revelation chapter 11:3, 6 speaks concerning the two witnesses, "(v. 3) And I will give power unto my two witnesses, and they shall prophesy a thousand two hundred and threescore days, clothed in sackcloth. (v. 6) These have power to shut heaven, that it rain not in the days of their prophecy [Elijah, I Kings 17, 18]: and have power over waters to turn them to blood [Moses, Exodus 4, 7], and to smite the earth with all plagues, as often as they will."

The OT informs us that Moses lacked the ability to "speak well"; thereby, God chose Aaron, the high priest, to speak God's message unto the people. In the OT, Aaron took the rod and hit the water turning it to blood. Aaron's presence in this OT picture signifies to us today that the other witness who shall come in the spirit and power of Moses turning the water to blood will *lack* the office of a high priest, the *mouth-piece*. Therefore of the two prophets, Moses and Elias, if ye will receive it, *this is the voice* of the one that crieth in the wilderness. Prepare ye the way for the coming of Christ. As the Word says in John chapter 1:5, "And the *light shineth in darkness*; and the darkness comprehended it not." This voice that crieth in the wilderness *is not that Light*, but has come to bare witness of that Light. I was but a chosen vessel unto God's service. I could do nothing without hearing the voice of God and doing the will of the Father. To God be *all* the glory.

Special recognitions:

- This book also comes to you through the loving hands of Karyn Keyser whom the Lord has chosen to type the many drafts of this manuscript. Karyn's hard work and dedication is to be honored and highly commended.
- To my wonderful husband Michael Barclay and children: Adam, Jared, Michael, and John for their loving support.
- To my mother, Juanita McPeak, who through her love and discipline helped to shape and mold my very being.

Recognitions to those who gave moral support and or financial support:
- To my sister Elaine who led me to Christ and her husband Brad Crowder, both whom supported me during this endeavor.
- To my brother Erick McPeak for all of his encouragement and support.
- To my best of friends Bill and Linda Clinton.
- To Karyn's husband David Keyser.

Recognitions to others:
- To my eldest brother Mark McPeak who helped to support the family in the absence of our father.
- To my brother Gary McPeak for being the "big brother" I always needed.

I love you all, and may God bless
each and everyone of you.

Editor: Jan Ballentine

ISRAEL'S PRIME MINISTER = 666
(Benjamin Netanyahu is the Antichrist)

Netanyahu has temporarily lost his seat, but his deadly wound to his headship, or leadership, shall be healed, Rev. 13:2, 3.

Revelation 13:16-18, "And he causeth *all*...to receive a mark in their right hand, or in their foreheads: And that no man might buy or sell, save he that had the mark, or the name of the beast, or the number of his **_name_**...it is the number of a **man**; and his number is six hundred threescore and six" (666).

Revelation 14, "If any man...receive his mark...The same shall drink of the wine of the wrath of God...and he shall be tormented with fire and brimstone...for ever."

Name in the Greek means **_authority_**

Netanyahu received his authority on:

*He became Prime Minister on the Jew's 6th day or Friday.	*He was not sworn into office, to rule the nation, until the 6th month.	*He began to rule and reign in the 6th year or 1996.

THE NUMBER TO HIS NAME OR WHEN HE
RECEIVED HIS AUTHORITY IS 666!

Jesus said, "Marvel not...Ye must be born again."
Here's how: Acts 2:38

xviii

To order the book, *Christ Is Coming; the Antichrist Is Revealed*, send a donation of $15.00 or more to: ENDTIME CRUSADERS, Inc., P.O. Box 1035, Safety Harbor, FL 34695, or order it through the internet http://www.1stbooks.com.

A COPY OF THE OFFICIAL REGISTRATION AND FINANCIAL INFORMATION MAY BE OBTAINED FROM THE DIVISION OF CONSUMER SERVICES BY CALLING TOLL-FREE WITHIN THE STATE. REGISTRATION DOES NOT IMPLY ENDORSEMENT, APPROVAL, OR RECOMMENDATION BY THE STATE. 1-800-435-7352.

ENDTIME CRUSADERS, INC.

God is bringing His endtime message to the world to regain what Satan has stolen!
Benjamin Netanyahu, Israel's Prime Minister, is the Antichrist = 666!

Concerning the day of Christ: II Thess. 2 states, "Let no man deceive you by any means, for that day shall not come, except . . . that man of sin be revealed, the *son of perdition*."

Judas (John 17:12) & the Antichrist (II Thess. 2) are the only two in the entire Bible titled the son of perdition. The reason ---
Judas' past is the key to the Antichrist's future.

Judas	Antichrist
John 13:2, 21-27 = His heart was to betray Christ. He spoke lies at the table (took sop) & received 30 pieces of silver.	Da. 11:27, 28 = His heart is to do mischief. He speaks lies at the table (strikes deal betraying country), doesn't prosper (as with Judas, it will not pay off). He returns into his land with great riches. (Confirms a deal was made.)
John 2:19 = Jesus said, "DESTROY THIS TEMPLE, & in 3 days I will raise it up." Judas came with swords and staves (an army) to desecrate Jesus Christ, the temple of God.	Da. 11:31 = Antichrist takes away the daily sacrifice & places the abomination that maketh desolate. As the guide to an army, he shall desecrate the temple of God. II Thess. 2 says he sitteth in the temple of God.

<u>For Confirmation: Acts 1:16 ties together Psalms 109:6-8;</u>

1) Acts 1:16, "**Judas, which was guide to them that took Jesus.**"
2) Psalm 109:6-8, Holy Ghost by the mouth of David said, "**Let another take his office.**"
Two verses = Let another take his office, which was "guide" to them that took Jesus (temple). The Antichrist will take Judas' office as the guide to them that desecrate the temple. Judas was a betrayer; a betrayer plays two roles (apostle & guide)!

Benjamin Netanyahu will provide Israel's temple and then sit in it showing himself to be God!

CHRIST IS COMING; THE ANTICHRIST IS REVEALED
By: Debra Barclay

Chapter 1
Signs of the Times

What would happen if a hundred-mile-an-hour fast ball came straight at your face, and you ignored it? That's right; it would knock you out! The same is true if you ignore the warning signs God has provided for you in His Word. To get our attention focused on Him and off other things, the Lord has given certain danger signs that would precede His coming. We need to wake up! We need to take heed to His words and what is going on around us. God is at the door, and we are not looking at Him. Paul wrote in Romans 13:11, "And that, *knowing the time*, that now it is high time to *awake out of sleep*: for now is our salvation nearer than when we believed."

The Lord has warned us that in the last days perilous times would come. He compared the last days to the days of Lot. In recent days, troubles, famines, and earthquakes have occurred in various places marking the *__beginning birthing pains__*. These signs, *__combined with the rebirth of the nation of Israel in 1948__*, have sounded the alarm of the immanent return of Jesus Christ. However, as with a woman bearing a child, the *__real travail__* comes at the end. For when they shall cry peace and safety, then the Bible says there will be *"sudden destruction."*

Perilous Times

Surrounded by darkness, our world rapidly spins out of control. Moral corruption of the population is on the rise. People once valued things that we no longer consider important. The world is a 'live and let live' type of place where anything

goes. II Timothy 3:1-4 illustrates our generation for us:
(v. 1) This know also, that in the last days ***perilous times*** shall come. (v. 2) **For men shall be lovers of their own selves**, covetous, boasters, proud, blasphemers, disobedient to parents, unthankful, unholy, (v. 3) **Without natural affection,** . . . despisers of those that are good . . . (v. 4) lovers of pleasures more than lovers of God . . . .

Luke 17:28 says before the Son of Man is revealed, the world shall be " . . . as it was in the days of Lot . . . ." Abraham's nephew, Lot, chose to dwell in Sodom, due to the prosperity of the city. Sodom was "a city plagued by homosexuality or 'sodomy' (Genesis 19:5). Webster defines 'sodomy' as: unnatural sexual intercourse" (1). In the Old Testament, Leviticus 20:13 reads, "If a man also lie with mankind, as he lieth with a woman, both of them have committed an abomination: they shall surely be put to death." In the New Testament, homosexuality is still being condemned. Romans 1:27 states, "And likewise also the men, leaving the natural use of the woman, burned in their lust one toward another; men with men working that which is unseemly, and receiving in themselves that recompense of their error which was meet."

Sexual promiscuity and immorality have been around since the beginning of time; however, when I was growing up they were concealed in the closet. Today they are openly promoted everywhere. The media is full of sexual perversion. On national television, celebrities are blatantly discussing their homosexual lifestyles. Even those who claim to be priests have been exposed in the newspapers as gay. Never before in the history of time have we ever heard of legalizing gay marriages; yet in the last few years gay couples desiring to be married have pushed their way into our courtrooms. And what about gay rights in the military? Then there is Disney's promotion of "gay days" when Disney openly invites homosexuals to come out for the weekend.

Hey folks, it's just like it was in the days of Lot when men, burning with lust, stood outside Lot's own home and called for the two angels to come outside. When they did not conform to the sin, the men tried to push themselves inside. Sin is always knocking at our door; still we do not have to let it in. Romans

6:6 tells us " . . . we should not serve sin." Our Lord hates sin, but He loves the sinner. It does not matter where you have been or what you have done. God has made a way for you. He loves you, and He died for you. Even so, you must turn from your old ways, and obey the Word of God.

The Beginning Birthing Pains

Jesus spoke in Mark 13:8: ". . . and there shall be **earthquakes** in divers places, and there shall be **famines** and **troubles** [*DISTURBANCE*, i.e. (*OF WATER*) roiling (2)]: *these are the beginnings of sorrows*." 'Sorrows' in Greek means pangs, esp. of childbirth (3): "The Jewish people know about these birth pangs. Hebrew eschatology, called *acharit ha-yamin*, describes the *pre-Messianic era* as one of *great upheavals* and wars, known as 'the birth pangs of the Messiah . . . .'" (4). (These warning signs are also the preliminaries to the wrath the church will suffer, see Mark 13:8-9.) Our earth has awakened out of her sleep due to the beginning of sorrows.

If you feel skeptical that the following birthing pains are trying to warn us of the Messiah's coming, then maybe it is because you are not aware of the conditions. However, as with a woman bearing a child, the beginning experience sometimes goes unnoticed. Even so, with time, the pains will become more apparent as the contractions increase and intensify prior to the peek of the birth. For evidence of the earth's contractions, just watch the news or read the papers! Newspaper reports with comments such as the following have become an epidemic around the world:

1) "Grand Forks, N.D. – With icy water lapping at roof tops, President Clinton flew by helicopter above this flooded city . . . and pledged nearly half a billion dollars to help Red River victims 'in the fight of their lives' . . . . 'I have never seen a community this inundated by flood . . . . We do not know . . . for sure that the warming of the Earth is responsible for what seems to be a **substantial increase in highly disruptive weather events**', [stated President Clinton]" (5). Grand Forks had record flooding.

3

2) Clinton was quoted in another article saying, "'I think every American has noticed a substantial increase in the last few years** of the kind of thing we're going to see in North Dakota today . . . . And just let me say in closing, with regard to the comments he (Vice President) made about climate change and the possible impact it may have had on **the enormous number of highly disruptive weather** events that have occurred just since we've been here in the last 4 years and a few months . . .'" (6).

3) "On balance, the planet is in trouble . . . . Worldwatch says a worsening global climate is at the root of grain shortages and predicted food price increases . . . . The world grain harvest was the smallest since 1988 and grain reserves - the grain available to the world if all production stopped - were at an all-time low of just 48 days of consumption" (7).

4) "Hurricane Bertha ripped up . . . tobacco crop, mulched acres of his soybeans, and pressed tall stalks of corn into the dirt. But Hurricane Fran's winds . . . shucked the golden ears right on the stalk. 'I've never seen anything like this in 40 years of farming . . . ' [stated a local farmer in North Carolina] . . . . There is little left of North Carolina's $20 billion agricultural industry . . . " (8).

5) "El Nino Spawns Weird Events; Seafood Businesses Suffering" (9). El Nino, 1997, was the most intense warming ever recorded.

6) "'Storms hit Midwest' [-] The worst flooding in Chicago-area history turned streets into rivers" (10).

7) "Last year was the busiest Atlantic hurricane season in 60 years . . . causing $7.7 billion in damages" (11).

8) ". . . the number of earthquakes recorded has risen from 2,588 in 1983 to 4,084 in 1992" (12).

9) "The 'Blizzard of '96' . . . appeared . . . likely to be one of the greatest of the 20th century in the urban Northeast" (13).

10) "Record snow and cold plagued central and eastern states during the 1995-96 winter, setting seasonal and annual snowfall records from Minnesota to New England" (14).

11) "In some spots from Oklahoma to Arizona, the dryness from fall into late spring was as severe as any observed this

century, including the Dust Bowl years . . . . The drought dealt agriculture a multibillion-dollar blow . . . . 'It caught us right in the heart of the winter wheat cycle,' said Howard Johnson, Oklahoma's associate state climatologist for service" (15).

12) In 1995, about 700 people lost their lives from a heat wave in Chicago. The city of Chicago has never seen such a disaster as this.

13) "High water and mudslides closed major roads in California, Idaho, Nevada, Oregon and Washington, where 70 counties have been declared disaster areas since a nonstop string of storms began Dec. 26; . . . damage is in the hundreds of millions of dollars" (16).

14) "A bad year in America's Midwestern breadbasket has Kneece and other South Carolina farmers looking to reap huge profits from the skyrocketing prices of corn . . . . With more rain than normal this spring, many Midwestern farmers have not been able to get into their fields. And a drought in the Southwest has cut into the corn crop there" (17).

15) "The Oklahoma agriculture commissioner, Dennis Howard, predicted last week that 5,000 to 10,000 of the state's 70,000 farming families would go bankrupt this year because of the drought and record low cattle prices brought on by mass liquidation of some ranchers' herds. Howard said half the farm families in the state were in 'critical financial shape'" (18).

16) A local farmer in Indiana stated, "'I'm 74, and this is the worst year I've seen in my life . . . '" (19).

17) Starvation is on the rise in places such as Rwanda, Zaire, Haiti, North Korea, and it goes on and on.

The increase in natural disasters taking place will eventually bring about great consequences. I have read countless articles and seen innumerable news reports explaining that billions of dollars have been spent in an effort to help relieve various cities, counties even other countries, struck by these occurrences. The *world* cannot afford to bear their heavy burden. While running rapidly toward the finish line of a one world government and one world religion, it is my belief these natural phenomena will be responsible for the final thrust to get us across that line.

Israel 1948

Why now? How do we know this is the time in which the
Lord will return?

In Genesis 12.2, 3, we read of the various blessings God
gave to Abraham. Of the promises, one was related to the
coming of the Messiah through the *seed* of Abraham; verse 7
adds, "Unto thy seed will I give this land [Canaan/Israel]." God
gave the Promised Land to the Jews; thus, Gen. 21:12 states, ". .
. for in Isaac shall thy seed be called." The Lord confirmed His
promises with a blood covenant, and He alone passed through
the divided halves of animals (Gen. 15). Normally when making
a covenant both parties would be required to pass between the
halves of the animals, but in this case, Abraham was simply put
to sleep. God was making it clear He would keep His promise
regardless of Abraham's or his descendants' actions (see also
Hebrews 6:17).

Although it is true throughout time that God has expelled the
Hebrew people from their homeland as a form of punishment, it
is not true that He has forsaken them. Portraying history's end,
many of the Old Testament prophets saw into the distant future a
time when God would keep His promises and bring Israel back
into her homeland. Then in 1948 the miracle happened; Israel
became a nation in the fulfillment of God's Word. Isaiah writes
in 11:10, "And in that day there shall be a root of Jesse, which
shall stand for an ensign of the people; to it shall the Gentiles
seek: and his rest shall be glorious." The Messiah is called "the
root of Jesse." Jesse was David's father, and David was the king
of Israel's twelve tribes. Jesus Christ came through the lineage
of David. As the root of Jesse, He contains Israel's sap and
strength, *giving life to them as a nation*. This whole message of
Isaiah 11:10-12 could not have been fulfilled until after the time
of Christ's death. Through the root of Jesse, all the nations shall
find rest.

Isaiah 11:11 continues, "And it shall come to pass in that
day, that the Lord shall set his hand again the *second time* to

6

recover the remnant of his people, which shall be left, from Assyria, and from Egypt, and from Pathros, and from Cush, and from Elam, and from Shinar, and from Hamath, and from the islands of the sea." This verse speaks of Israel's redemption. We know we are living in "that day" because of the words "second time." *Prophesy in the News* writes in its July 1996 issue,

> Isaiah wrote in the days before the Babylonian captivity, but he did not simply write that the Lord will set his hand to recover the remnant of His people. He went beyond that. He saw a second dispersion of the Jews from their land and wrote that 'in that day the Lord shall set His hand AGAIN the SECOND time' . . . . The rebirth of the nation of Israel in 1948 marked the second return of the Jews to their land . . . [when] the people were led into Babylonian captivity, and when they returned, they returned from Babylon [and without independence]. But in that day designated for the far future, the Israeli people will return from many lands. (20)

Isaiah 11:12 states, "And he shall set up an ensign for the nations, and shall assemble the outcasts of Israel, and gather together the dispersed of Judah from the four corners of the earth." This tells us an ensign for the nations would be the assembling of Israel and a gathering of Judah from all four corners of the world.

Jeremiah 23:7, 8 states,

> (v. 7) Therefore, behold, the days come, saith the LORD, that they shall no more say, The LORD liveth [give life; nourish up (21)], which brought up the children of Israel out of the land of Egypt; (v. 8) But, The LORD liveth, which brought up and which led the seed of the house of Israel out of the north country, and from all countries whither I had driven them; and they shall dwell in their own land.

Coming out of Egypt, God **nourished** the Israelites "**giving life**" through *Manna*. As in Isaiah chapter 11 verses 10-12, Jesus Christ, the Manna in John chap. 6, has once again "**given life**" to Israel as a nation. (Note: in the Babylonian and Maccabee period, the manna had not come down from heaven yet; however, Isaiah 11 and Jeremiah 23 both center around the one who "gives life," the bread of life, Jesus Christ.) Like Jeremiah has stated, He has brought them up (or made them a nation); now He is leading the Jews back from Russia and around the world into their homeland.

How do we know this is the time of the Lord's immanent return? The parable of the fig tree tells us the story. The fig tree symbolizes the nation of Israel: "The Gospels tell us that Jesus cursed a barren fig tree whose leafiness suggested fruitfulness (Mk. 11:13, 14, 20, 21). Most scholars view this fig tree as a symbol of Israel, which in Jesus' day appeared to be vital but was actually barren of righteousness (compare Mk. 11:15-19; Isa. 5:1-7)" (22).

Jesus taught in Matthew 24:32, 33, "(v. 32) Now learn a parable of the fig tree; When his branch is yet tender, and *putteth forth leaves*, ye know that *summer* is nigh: (v. 33) So *likewise* ye, when ye shall *SEE all these things*, know that it is near, even at the doors." God is telling us when we "*look upon*" a tree and notice the *growth* of its leaves, we should know the season. Therefore, a tree is something that shows the season to us.

Now compare this to Luke 21:29, 30, "(v. 29) . . . Behold the *fig tree, and* all the trees [or "these things" that show the season spoken of in Matt. 24]; (v. 30) When they now shoot forth [or like the leaves in the previous passage, *they grow*], ye *see* and know of your own selves that summer is now nigh at hand." When we *see* the fig tree, which is the birth of Israel in 1948, *coming together* with all the trees or these things that show the season, such as earthquakes, famines, and troubles, then we know that the coming of the Lord is near.

The establishment of Israel as a nation has happened *along with* an increased growth in the number of natural disasters. Scripture warns, "(v. 31) . . .when ye see these things come to pass, know ye that the kingdom of God is nigh at hand. (v. 32) Verily I say unto you, This generation shall not pass away, till all be fulfilled" (Luke 21:31, 32).

8

The Real Travail

When I was a teenager, I had always heard there would be a peace treaty signing between the Palestinians and the Jews. This was to be a significant sign of the Lord's return. Micah 3:5 states, "Thus saith the LORD concerning the prophets that make my people err, that bite with their teeth, and *cry, Peace; and he that putteth not into their mouths, they even prepare war against him.*" Before the world's cameras, on Monday, September 13, 1993, an historical moment took place. A somewhat reluctant Prime Minster, Yitzhak Rabin, and the covetous Palestinian Liberation Organization (PLO) Chairman, Yasser Arafat, shook hands becoming partners for peace. President Clinton brought together Israeli Prime Minister Yitzhak Rabin and PLO Chairman Yasser Arafat, both of which had been on opposite sides of an ongoing bloody battle.

At this event, **all three leaders used God's Word to obtain support from the people for their decision in trading God's land for peace, but He did not put it into their mouths**. In an attempt to tie this moment into a biblical perspective, President Clinton stated,

> "*The children of Abraham, the descendants of Isaac and Ishmael*, have embarked together on a bold journey. Together, today, with all our hearts and all our souls, we bid them, 'Shalom, salaam, peace' . . . . The sound we heard today, once again as in ancient Jericho, was of trumpets toppling walls . . . . This time, praise God, the trumpets herald not the destruction of that city but its new beginning . . . ." (23)

Yasser Arafat in his opening remarks stated, "'*In the name of God*, the most merciful and compassionate . . . [n]ow as we stand on the threshold of this new historic era, . . . [o]ur two peoples are awaiting today this historic hope, and they want to give peace a real chance . . . . [T]he land of peace, the land of peace yearns for a just and comprehensive peace'" (24).

Prime Minister Yitzhak Rabin stated,

> "This signing of the Israeli-Palestinian declaration of

9

principles here today, it's not so easy, neither for myself as a soldier in Israel's war, nor for the people of Israel, nor for the Jewish people in the Diaspora who are watching us now with great hope mixed with apprehension . . . . We have come from Jerusalem, the . . . *eternal capital* of the Jewish people . . . . Let me say to you, the Palestinians . . . [e]nough of blood and tears . . . . We are today giving peace a chance and saying to you . . . enough. [O]ur higher moral values have been derived for thousands of years from the *Book of the Books*, in one of which, Koheleth, we read, 'To every thing there is a season and a time to every purpose *under heaven* . . . . A time to be born and a time to die, a time to kill and ***a time to heal*** . . . a time of war and a time of peace' . . . the time for peace has come . . . ." (25)

"*A time to heal*," Jeremiah 8:11 speaks of that day: "For they have ***healed*** the hurt of the daughter of my people slightly, saying, '***Peace, peace; when there is no peace.***'" It's no secret that PLO Chairman Yasser Arafat has a mouth that speaks both ways. To the west, he speaks of peace on the lawn of the White House. To his people, he speaks of the war, Jihad. *Jerusalem Post* editor Bar-Illan stated: "'. . . [Arafat wants to] get as much territory as possible through peace or some kind of agreement, and then, when Israel is dwarfed and becomes very small and vulnerable, then - and only then - attack it . . . giving it the final blow'" (26). Arafat makes statements of war:

"A young child of the uprising [one who is against Israeli occupation] will raise the flag of Palestine on the minarets of Jerusalem, on the churches of Jerusalem. Jerusalem will be the capital of the Palestinian state, whether anyone else likes it or not," Arafat told 3,000 cheering supporters at a refugee camp on the Gaza strip. At a gathering in Gaza to memorialize slain Fatah leaders, Arafat said: "All of us are willing to be martyrs on our way to Jerusalem - the capital of Palestine . . . . In the end, we will fly the Palestinian flag over the walls of Jerusalem." (27)

The day of the LORD'S visitation is quickly approaching us. I Thessalonians 5:2, 3 reminds us: "(v. 2) For yourselves know perfectly that the day of the Lord so cometh as a thief in the night. (v. 3) For when they shall say, *Peace and safety*; then *sudden destruction* cometh upon them, *as travail* upon a woman with child; and they shall not escape." According to *Strong's Exhaustive Concordance*, the word "safety" in this verse means security (28). Interestingly enough, Israel's Prime Minister Benjamin Netanyahu ran his campaign slogan on the words, "NETANYAHU - WE WILL BRING PEACE AND SECURITY." In Ezekiel 38:11 the Hebrew root to security is translated in the KJV as safety (29). To put it plainly, *Netanyahu's slogan proclaimed "Peace and Safety."*

To understand the significance of what is taking place here, Israel selling out her land for peace, we must begin with the Word of God. In Gen. 15, God gave the land of Canaan to the Jews for an inheritance. Leviticus 25:23 establishes, *"The land shall not be sold [to surrender (30)] for ever*: for the land is mine; for ye are strangers and sojourners with me." Jerusalem is God's Holy Land in the sense it has been set aside for God's service to fulfill prophecies. In the book of Micah, God warns the Israeli leaders of oppressing a man and taking his heritage from him. Yet these leaders, because the power was in their hands, have taken God out of the picture to create their own man-made kingdom, and because of this God's judgement shall surely come.

Chapter 2
Christ Is Coming

For centuries, the church has been looking for the Second Coming of Christ, which will mark the beginning of our eternal salvation. The Bible describes this glorious event in I Thessalonians 4:16, 17: "(v. 16) For the Lord himself shall descend from heaven with a shout, with the voice of the archangel, and with the trump of God: and the dead in Christ shall rise first: (v. 17) Then we which are alive and remain shall be caught up together with them in the clouds, to meet the Lord in the air: and so shall we ever be with the Lord." The *Thompson Chain Reference Bible* refers to the above scripture and II Thessalonians 2:1 as the Second Coming of Christ.

Paul elaborates more on Christ's Second Coming in II Thessalonians chapter 2. He gives the church some added signs to look for prior to the return of Christ. One of the signs is the man of sin, the Antichrist, will be revealed. However, many people are under the misconception that the church will be raptured, or caught up to meet the Lord in the air, prior to this event happening, but this is not the case. Pay close attention to the word **"revealed"** used on three different occasions in II Thess. 2:1-8:

> (v. 1) Now we beseech you, brethren, by the coming of our Lord Jesus Christ, and by our gathering together unto him, (v. 2) That ye be not **soon** shaken in mind, or be troubled, neither by spirit, nor by word, nor by letter as from us, as that the day of Christ is at hand. (v. 3) *Let no man deceive you by any means*: for that day shall not come, **except** there come a falling away first, and *__that man of sin be revealed__*, the son of perdition; (v. 4) Who opposeth and exalteth himself above all that is called God, or that is worshipped; so that he as God sitteth in the temple of God, shewing himself that he is God. (v. 5) Remember ye not, that, when I was yet with you, I told you *these things*? (v. 6) And now ye know what withholdeth that he might be **revealed _in his time_**. (v. 7) For the mystery of iniquity

doth already work: only he who now letteth will let, until he be taken out of the way. (v. 8) And then shall that Wicked be **revealed**, whom the Lord shall consume with the spirit of his mouth, and shall destroy with the brightness of his coming.

This is where I stopped reading and said, "Now, wait a second, Lord. You said the church would not be gathering together unto you until the man of sin be revealed to them (see verse 3). However, here in verse 8 you are saying the Wicked is going to be "revealed" when you consume him at your coming. What do you mean here, for this sounds like a contradiction?" The Lord then helped me to understand **the first "revealed" in verse 3 is to the *brethren* (note: vs. 1). The word "revealed" in verse 8 is to the *world*.**

From verses 1 to 7, God was speaking to the church. He let us know before His Second Coming the "man of sin" must be **revealed** to us. Then in verse 8, He describes how the Wicked will be revealed unto the **world** when the Lord comes down and consumes him. Imagine that! People in this world will be bowing down worshiping what they believe to be God, when all of a sudden the Lord will come forth in all of His power and glory to destroy the Antichrist. In total shock, the world will then realize he was not God after all. Notice in the Word of God how Paul segregated the church and spoke to them in verses 1-7. He then also spoke of the world in verses 7-12. Hence, verses 7 and 8 concern the Antichrist; verse 9, the false prophet; and verses 10-12, the people in the world who associate with these two evil men.

To further prove the Antichrist will be revealed unto us, look at verse 5: "Remember ye not, that, when I was yet with you, I told you **these things**?" Paul was asking the church to recall the ***order of God's given events***. The Lord has a plan, and ***His plan has an order.*** Everything in verses 1-4 has mentioned an appointed time. Notice the "**things**" Paul mentioned: First he told the church not to be **"soon"** shaken. In other words, do not concern yourself church; it's not going to happen in "**your time**." He then gives the church their answer in verse 3, ". . . *for* **that day** *shall not come*, ___except___ . . . "; again, there is an

14

appointed time even for Christ's coming. Now some will tell you God could come at any time, but this statement is contrary to His Word. The Word specifically says the day of Christ **shall not come** *except these things* precede His coming.

Watch how Paul puts these events in a sequential order according to time;

- *"First,"* there must be a falling away (a rebellion NIV).
- **Also, the man of sin is revealed, the son of perdition**.
- The Antichrist as God sitteth in the temple of God.

THE *REVELL BIBLE DICTIONARY* **STATES, ". . . 2 TH. 2:3 PREDICTS A TIME OF APOSTASY OR** *REBELLION* **('FALLING AWAY', KJV)** *WHEN* **THE ANTICHRIST IS REVEALED"** (1). "Let *no man* deceive you by any means"; the **SON OF PERDITION must be revealed** at a time that will proceed Christ's coming. As we will see in the story of Judas, the title "son of perdition" is the major clue that helps unlock the door to the identity of this mystery man. Verse 4 then details information about the Antichrist sitting in the temple of God, and this is yet *another event* in time that must transpire before the day of Christ. *"These things*," referred to by Paul in verse 5, are the events which will precede the coming of Christ.

In Verse 6, "And **now** ye know what withholdeth that he [the man of sin, **the son of perdition**] might be revealed in **his time**." Paul is saying, **"now," right now without saying another word**, you should know what is keeping the son of perdition, **who precedes Christ's immanent return**, from being revealed. What is withholding the son of perdition from being unveiled is an APPOINTED TIME, *"his time*," mentioned in verse 6, given only by God. God is going to allow Satan to have his time during which Satan will plan his own sequence of events before the Lord's return.

The word "revealed," used in verses 3, 6, and 8 refers to the Antichrist, the *son of perdition*, being uncovered at a certain time. Remember in verses 1-7, he is being revealed to the church, and in verses 7-12, he is being revealed to the world. Verse 7 continues on with the thought of the Antichrist being revealed, and it confirms **"he"** in verse 6 refers to the son of perdition. Verse 7 reads, **"FOR THE MYSTERY OF**

INIQUITY *DOTH ALREADY WORK*." Paul is saying here that the mystery of iniquity is nothing new. The son of perdition, spoken of from verses 3 on down, is nothing new. Satan's plan has been in effect for a long time. The devil possessed Judas Iscariot to try to accomplish his goal, and he will do the same with this man.

Again, Judas and this man of sin are called the son of perdition. The son of perdition is discussed in great detail on pages 51-52. The devil has traveled this road for a long time now, but "his time" of a final destination will arrive soon. Verse 7 states, "only he who now letteth will let, until he be taken out of the way."

- The he in this verse is Satan.
- Letteth in the Greek means, keep (in memory), possess (2).
- Let in the Greek means, possess (3).

In other words, only Satan, who now *keeps in memory his plan to possess* will *possess* the son of perdition, until Satan is taken out of the way. The serpent incarnated in this man shall deceive the world, but only for a time.

SATAN'S WRATH (Revelation 12)

When Satan moves into his final position, this will be a time of great tribulation. The time of great tribulation the world will face is not God's wrath; *it is Satan's wrath*. The church is not appointed to God's wrath; however, it is appointed to Satan's wrath. Some of you may say, "Satan's wrath? I have never heard of that." Many people have not, but it is mentioned in Revelation chapter 12.

In this chapter, the Word speaks of a woman clothed with the **sun** with the **moon** under her feet and upon her head a crown of **twelve stars**. *The woman is Israel*; the twelve stars are the twelve tribes of Israel. This becomes evident when looking at Genesis 37. In this chapter, the same terms are being used: *sun, moon and stars*. In Gen. 37:9-10, Joseph, Jacob's son, represented one of the stars and the other eleven stars that were mentioned in this verse represented his eleven brothers. Thereby, you have the **twelve stars** or twelve tribes of Israel.

The woman in Revelation 12:1 is Israel, and the man-child in 12:5 is Jesus Christ. Jesus Christ "who was to rule all nations with a *rod of iron* . . . was caught up unto God, and to his throne," (Psalms 2:7-9; Rev. 19:15-16; see also pgs. 120-121).

Revelation 12:7-9 states, "(v. 7) And there was *war in heaven*: Michael and his angels fought against the dragon; and the dragon fought and his angels, (v. 8) And prevailed not; neither was their place found "*any more*" in heaven. (v. 9) And the great dragon was cast out, that old serpent, called the Devil, and Satan, which deceiveth the whole world: he was cast out into the earth, and his angels were cast out with him." Some people believe this war occurred before the creation of man. However, verses 10 and 11 discredit this idea: "(v. 10) . . . for the accuser of our *brethren* is cast down, which accused them before our God day and night. (v. 11) And **they overcame him by the blood of the Lamb**, and by the word of their testimony; and *they loved not their lives unto the death*." How can the devil be cast down before the creation, when he was in heaven accusing the "brethren"? He accuses the **brethren** before God day and night, just as he did with Job (Job ch. 1:6-12). *Once Satan* is kicked out of heaven and confined to this earth, the Word *then* states the blood of the Lamb saves us. Meaning, Jesus was *already* crucified on earth before Satan was cast out of heaven. Therefore, there is no way the devil was cast out before the creation of man.

When the serpent is thrown to the earth, Rev. 12:12 warns, "Woe to the inhabiters of the earth and of the sea! for the **devil** is come down unto you, having **great wrath**, because **he knoweth** that "*he hath*" but a short time [his time II Thess. 2:6]." When Satan is cast to the earth, he will enter Israel's Prime Minister Benjamin Netanyahu, the man of sin, the son of perdition. It will be "his time," *Satan's time of wrath*.

During the reign of the Antichrist, natural and spiritual Israel will be under intense persecution. Concerning natural Israel Rev. 12:6 states, "And the woman [natural Israel] fled into the wilderness, where she hath a place prepared of God, that *they should feed her there a thousand two hundred and threescore days*." There are two witnesses that will feed *natural Israel* for

17

this same exact number of days. Rev. 11:3, 7, 8 helps us understand this:

> (v. 3) And I will give power unto my two witnesses, and they shall _prophesy a thousand two hundred and threescore days_, clothed in sackcloth. (v. 7) And when they shall have finished their testimony, the beast that ascendeth out of the bottomless pit shall make war against them, and shall over-come them, and kill them. (v. 8) And their dead bodies shall lie in the street of the great city, which spiritually is called Sodom and Egypt, where also our Lord was crucified [natural Israel].

Truly, the woman in Rev. 12:6 is natural Israel because in Rev. 11 the two witnesses _are feeding_ natural Israel for the same 1,260-day period. Moreover, these two witnesses are then killed in Israel's streets.

Farther on in Rev. 12, spiritual Israel is also being persecuted. Rev. 12:13 states, "And when the dragon saw that he was cast unto the earth, he persecuted the woman [spiritual Israel - the church] which brought forth the _man child_." The man-child here is a _body of believers_ that are formed in the _image_ of Christ. Jesus Christ, the "man child" in Rev. 12:5, will rule the nations with a rod of iron, as will the church in Rev. 2:26, 27 because God made man in His own _image_. Romans 1:20 states, "For the _invisible_ things of him from the creation of the world are _clearly seen_, being understood _by the things that are made_, even his eternal power and Godhead; so that they are without excuse" (see also, I Cor. 11:7; James 3:9).

**Continuing on, this woman who brought forth the man-child did so to bring forth a seed**. Rev. 12:14, 17 states,

> (v. 14) And to the woman [the church] were given two wings of a great eagle, that she might fly into the wilderness, into her place, where she is nourished for a time, and times, and half a time, from the face of the serpent. (v. 17) And the dragon was wroth with the woman, and went to make war with the _remnant of her seed_ [the man child who will _come out_ from the woman], which keep the commandments of God, and have the testimony of Jesus Christ."

18

God, in these last days, is going to *call out* leaders from among the sheep to lead Israel just as He had done with David in II Samuel 7:8. Christ in Matthew ch. 17, called Peter, James and John up to a *high mountain apart* from the other apostles and church. Jesus gave these three men a vision of something the others could not see. Similarly, the believers, who know the times, who keep the commandments of God, and who have the testimony of Jesus Christ, shall instruct many. "[T]he testimony of Jesus is the spirit of prophecy" according to Rev. 19:10. Daniel 11:32-33 teaches that during this endtime persecution, "(v. 32) . . . the people that do know their God shall be strong, and do exploits. (v. 33) And they that understand *among the people* shall instruct many."

Another notable difference between the woman in Rev. 12:6 and the woman in Rev. 12:14 is the feeding time. The woman in Rev. 12:6 is being fed for a shorter period of time because the two witnesses, who feed natural Israel, will prophesy for 1,260 days. Yet the woman, spiritual Israel, in Rev. 12:14 will be nourished for a time, times, and a dividing of times or 42 months (Rev. 13:5-7). There are 17 days of difference in their feeding time.

Jesus warned of this same time of trouble in Matthew chapter 24. While sitting upon the Mount of Olives, Jesus with His disciples was looking down upon the second temple and discussing it. Our Lord stated in Matthew 24:2, "There shall not be left here one stone upon another, that shall not be thrown down." The disciples inquired in verse 3, ". . . when shall these things be? and *what shall be the sign of thy coming*, and of the end of the world?" Jesus then went on to answer their questions, and in verse 15 He gives one "**major sign**" before His return: "When ye therefore shall see the **abomination of desolation**, *spoken of by Daniel the prophet*, stand in the holy place, (whoso readeth, let him understand:)." While studying endtime prophecy, I discovered that: "When Jesus spoke of the Abomination of Desolation, he referred back to Daniel. However, Jesus included an additional piece of information not given in Daniel. He said the Abomination of Desolation would stand in the holy place" (4).

Remember that they were looking down upon the second temple, and in those days, the holy place was in the temple of God. Jesus was telling them the man of sin, the son of perdition, would stand in the holy place. We know this because Paul spoke of the same event in II Thessalonians 2:4. In this scripture, the son of perdition sits in the temple of God claiming to be God. In Matthew 24 and II Thessalonians, the last "**major sign**" occurring before the coming of Christ is this event. Once this event happens, Jesus states in Matthew 24:16, "**Then** let them which be in Judea flee into the mountains . . . (v. 21) **FOR THEN SHALL BE *GREAT TRIBULATION*.**" Jesus was saying, when you see the Abomination of Desolation stand in the holy place **then** flee because this is the time of great tribulation; the great tribulation will be Satan's time, his wrath. Directly after the great tribulation, God's judgement will occur:

> Matthew 24:29 teaches us this, "*__Immediately after the tribulation__* of those days shall the sun be darkened, and the moon shall not give her light, and the stars shall fall from heaven, and the powers of heavens shall be shaken." The sun being darkened, the moon being turned to blood, and the stars falling from heaven are all things that happen when the great day of **God's wrath** comes (Revelation 6:12-17) (5).

The Antichrist will have his time to rule and reign from the temple of God for three and a half years. Study Daniel 9:27, which says, "And he [the Antichrist] shall confirm the covenant with many for one week [a seven-year period]: and in the *midst* of the week he shall cause the sacrifice and the oblation to cease, and for the overspreading of abominations he shall make it desolate." The Antichrist will *confirm*, or strengthen by being in agreement with an already existing treaty. His approval will trigger the final seven-year period that will usher in the return of our Messiah. It is said Daniel's one week period is equal to seven years because:

1) In the **MIDST** or the middle of the week, the Antichrist shall be against the holy covenant. He shall then place the abomination of desolation; therefore, he shall stand in the holy place and call himself God (see Ex. 26:12 on pgs. 99-100).

20

2) When this event transpires, Jesus in Matthew 24:15 referred to Daniel and then said in verse 21, "[t]hen shall be great tribulation . . . ." It will be given unto Satan to make war with the saints for a three and a half-year period.

    A) Daniel 7:25, "And he shall speak great words against the most High, and shall wear out the saints of the most High, and think to change times and laws: and they shall be given into his hand until **a time** and **times** and the **dividing of time**." We know this is a three and a half-year period because of the information provided in the next verse.

    B) Revelation 13:5-7 tells us the Antichrist shall wear out the saints of the most High for 42 months, which equals three and a half years.

    C) Revelation 12:14 states, "And to the woman were given two wings of a great eagle, that she might fly into the wilderness, into her place, where she is nourished for time, and times, and half a time, from the face of the serpent."

3) Therefore since the last half of Daniel's one-week period is a three and a half-year period, then that means the first half is also a three and a half-year period. Some believe during the first three and a half years, the Antichrist ascends through peace and diplomacy as is shown in chapter 3.

    NOTE: *How do we know that Revelation 12:12, speaking of Satan's wrath, applies to Matthew 24 and our day?*

Well, Revelation 12:12-14 speaks of Satan's wrath being a three and a half-year period. This same theme of great tribulation with the same three and a half-year period occurs in all three texts: (Revelation 12:12-14, Da. 7:25, Matt. 24:15-16, 21). Even though Matthew did not specifically mention the three and a half-year period, Jesus referred us to Daniel who did mention it!

God will allow the Antichrist to have "his time" for several reasons. One of these is found in Daniel 12:9-10: "(v. 9) Go thy way, Daniel: for the words are closed up and sealed to the time of the end. (v. 10) **Many shall be purified**, and **made white**, and **tried**; but the wicked shall do wickedly: and none of the wicked shall understand; but the wise shall understand."

In an **appointed** time, God's people are going to be tried and purged to make them spiritually ready to meet their Messiah. Jesus spoke of one of the reasons for this cleansing. John 13:10-11 states, "(v. 10) He that is washed needeth not save to wash his feet, but is clean every whit: and ye are clean, **but not all**. (v. 11) For he knew who should betray him; therefore said he, **Ye are not all clean**." When the multitude came with Judas to capture Jesus, **the temple of God**, the sheep were then scattered. I believe there will be a reoccurrence of this situation. Sheep will scatter when God's people see this man desecrate the **temple of God** and claim to be the Messiah. However, out of all the apostles that followed Christ, only one was lost.

In these days, I am looking for a revival, a huge outpouring of the Holy Ghost. In Joel chapter 2:28, the Word informs us God is going to POUR out His Spirit. Nevertheless, you must keep a **purpose in your heart** not to bow down to the Antichrist or his image. In the days to come there will be a huge outpouring of the Holy Ghost, and there will also be an influx of demonic spirits. It will be a time of spiritual warfare. Satan with his angels will be kicked out of heaven, and evil spirits will also ascend from the bottomless pit. Folks, we need to be ready! Pastors, you have a huge responsibility to warn God's people. This message will prepare the hearts of saints and reach the lost. When the man of sin desecrates the temple, **Satan's wrath** is going to break loose, and we need to be ready for battle! This will be a time of great persecution, but through it, souls will be saved! Possibly your family member or the neighbor next door will not have to *burn forever* in the lake of fire where there is weeping and gnashing of teeth.

Let us not worry about ourselves, but let us think about the souls that are going to meet God. We must keep the kingdom of God in mind. God has a plan, and the church is on a journey. The church needs to adhere to the Father's will and follow the example of Jesus Christ, even if it means to our death. You might say, "Why would God do that to me?" Why did God allow it to happen to our Lord, to the apostles and to many other martyrs of the early church? Jesus said, "The servant is not greater than his lord. If they have persecuted me, they will also persecute you" (John 15:20). Do not worry! The Lord will not put anything more on us than we can bear. He has promised that!

Chapter 3
The Antichrist Is Revealed

One evening, while I was studying the Word, the Lord gave me the knowledge to understand some of the revelations in Daniel chapter 11. Excited, yet amazed, I ran to my husband, who was sitting in the front room, and said, "I know who the Antichrist is! God has revealed him to me!" Bewildered, my husband just watched and listened as I began to explain some of the following verses taken from this chapter.

> Daniel 11:19, Then he shall *turn his face* toward the *fort* of his own land: but he shall stumble and fall, and not be *found* [exist, present (1)].

The word "he" in this verse is Yitzhak Rabin, the former Israeli Prime Minister who took office on July 13, 1992. Instead of turning his face toward the enemy, Rabin *__turned it toward the fort (meaning the defense (2)) of his own land__*. In his article, "A Biblical Bird Disappears from the Israeli Landscape," Gary Stearman writes that "Prior to his assassination, Rabin had been branded a *moser* - a Hebrew term for one who collaborates with the enemy" (3). And he did just that. When he gave Israel's land to the enemy, he gave away their defense, for **the land acts as a *natural fort***. This God-given land separates them from their enemy. The further they are away from the opponent, the more military warning time they have in case of an attack. Notwithstanding, Yitzhak Rabin, instead of facing the adversary, "turned his face" in uniting with them, leaving him only to look back upon his people and their land.

Rabin had forgotten this sacred land did not belong to him. Setting God aside, he used his power of authority and signed an agreement with PLO leader Yasser Arafat. This agreement totally defied the Word of God. Outraged by his action, Yigal Amir, a religious nationalist and law student, murdered Rabin with two bullet wounds to the back. However terrible this may seem, "[s]ome evangelical Christians saw the event as part of

God's unfolding plan for Israel's destiny" (4). God raises up
leaders and brings them down. In the fulfillment of prophecy,
King David killed King Saul's assassin even though,
paradoxically, Saul's death paved the way for David to usurp
authority over Israel. Similarly, Yitzhak Rabin, who started to
build his own kingdom, pushed the Lord to the side and touched
what wasn't his, the land. Now he is no longer in *existence*. In
fulfillment of prophecy, Rabin's death, on November 4, 1995,
paved the way for the ascension of the next Israeli leader,
Shimon Peres.

> <u>Daniel 11:20</u>, **Then shall stand up in his estate a raiser of
> taxes . . . .**

1) **Taxes** - to drive, tax, tyrannize (5).
>   A) <u>Drive</u> - coerce, compel, instigate, push (6).
>   B) <u>Tax</u> - a heavy demand (7).
>   C) <u>Tyrannize</u> - to exercise arbitrary (willful, unwise, or
>   irrational choices (8)) power over (9).

After Rabin's assassination, Israeli Foreign Minister Shimon
Peres took his office. As a **"raiser of taxes,"** Peres was the
driving force behind the peace treaty signing. He was the one
who *coerced* Yitzhak Rabin into taking a step toward peace.
Shimon Peres didn't just broker the agreement, but he birthed it.
That is why he was commonly called the "architect of the
covenant."

Ido Dissentshik, an Israeli political commentator, sums it up
in his article titled, "Why Yitzhak Rabin Changed His Mind:"

> Rabin is a conservative person. He hates to change
> policies and attitudes. He is a systematic thinker but
> within carefully set frames. *__He is not a visionary like his
> foreign minister, Shimon Peres__*. Even his pragmatism is
> limited by a profound sense of suspicion. In particular he
> is suspicious of Peres, whom he once termed "a tireless
> saboteur." So the miracle in the breakthrough [why he
> changed his mind in meeting with Arafat] is even greater,
> because it was *__untrustworthy Peres the fantasizer who__*

not only led it but also "sold" it to Rabin as the only possible solution . . . . Rabin had reluctantly made Peres foreign minister, but with reduced status and authority to the point that he was not invited to sit in on meetings with visitors such as Secretary of State Warren Christopher. In March Peres had appeared ready to resign and fight. But his people reported to him that their secret negotiations (unknown to Rabin at the time) with the PLO were serious enough to warrant his patience. He was skeptical, but he allowed his deputy, Yossi Beilin, to go on. Only late in May or early June did he go to Rabin with a first draft of a Declaration of Principles. To his surprise, he was not fired but got a green light. (10)

Peres, a **"raiser of taxes**," the *driving force* behind giving away Israeli land for peace, also fits the definition of a *tyrant*. Displaying an unwise, irrational choice, Shimon Peres, "[a]gainst associates' advice, . . . insisted on putting forth his vision of a new Middle East of peace and cooperation between Israel and its Arab neighbors. 'He put a high priority on integration with the Arab world, and it appeared to be a *higher priority than security*. He kept talking about the new Middle East . . . . Most Israelis don't buy this' [Alpher stated]" (11). Peres' actions were seen as a *threat* to Israeli security, especially after a series of suicide bombings from militant Islamic groups. The Prime Minister Benjamin Netanyahu, commonly known as Bibi, then amplified the anxiety of the public by basing his campaign for the prime ministership on fear tactics, saying that Peres was unjust and reckless in his decision making policies. Netanyahu claimed he would bring Israel real peace and real security. Meir Shitrit, a relative dove commented, "'We must project ourselves as able to make a better peace than them - one that doesn't just *surrender everything*'" (12).

Yitzhak Rabin gave away the Israeli land, a biblical land, and then he paid for it with his life. Shimon Peres, as a "raiser of taxes," was the *driver* and *tyrant* behind it all. As the new Prime Minister, Shimon Peres picked up where Rabin left off. However, this time it would be in the glory of the kingdom.

<u>Daniel 11:20 continues</u>, Then shall stand up in his estate a raiser of taxes *in the glory of the kingdom* . . . .

Peres took office "**in the glory of the kingdom**" because at the time when he came in, Israel was in a state of national repentance. When Rabin was in office, the kingdom was divided on whether to give away land for peace. There was much turmoil in the region as the Islamic terrorists were willing to become martyrs to stop the peace process. As the death toll rose, the Jewish people feared for their lives and the lives of others.

Because of the numerous terrorist attacks, Israeli President Ezer Weizman called on Rabin to rethink the way they were headed. He then added they should stop the peace process. In January of 1995, Wilbur G. Landrey, foreign correspondent for the *St. Petersburg Times*, noted, "The newspaper Maariv reported that 50 percent of Israelis agree, and only 37 percent favored continuing - along with Rabin, whose own Cabinet is divided both on the process and the settlements" (13). Rabin's opponent, Netanyahu, added fuel to the fire with his constant outbursts against Rabin's decision to trade land for peace. In a rage, he shouted to a crowd, "'This government is opening the way to an Islamic Palestinian state in the suburbs of Jerusalem and Tel Aviv! . . . Never before in the history of Israel has any government conceded so much, so quickly - for nothing! Rabin has no right to endanger the state, to bury the Jewish dream of generations!'" (14). While Rabin was resuming peace talks in Washington, the Israelis became more and more divided. Thousands of people attended a protest, which was lead by Benjamin Netanyahu: "They wave[d] giant Israeli flags and desperate signs: 'Today the Golan, Tomorrow Jerusalem . . . Rabin Is Leading Us To Civil War . . . STOP THE SURRENDER'" (15).

Israel was in a time of turmoil as the country was undoubtedly divided over Rabin's decision to give away the land. Then suddenly, "Israeli opinion was turned upside down by the murder of Yitzhak Rabin" (16). A wave of anger and fear swept over the Jewish people. The nation was stunned as thoughts of "a Jew killing a Jew," haunted the minds and souls of many. "Thousands of Jews are asking: Who are we? Do we love each other or hate each other?" reported Peter Wallsten in the November 20, 1995, *St. Petersburg Times* (17). Remorse filled the land bringing many to a state of repentance. "'I'm sorry, I ask for forgiveness. If I spoke ill. If I uttered bad words. They were just words spoken in anger, in concern for the people of Israel,'" commented Eliezer Botavia, a resident of Kiryat Arba, a suburb of Hebron (18). Thousands filled the streets as mourning went on throughout the land. When all the graffiti came down overnight in Israel, it was proclaimed a "miracle."

The message now would be unity. The Times Wires suggested, "In the wake of the slaying by an opponent of Rabin's peace plan, *Israeli political leaders across the board* spoke only of how to mend the torn country" (19). **Undoubtedly, Peres came in "in the glory of the kingdom."** *He entered the kingdom at a time of a revolutionary mind set.* Law makers spanning the political spectrum were now coming together to demonstrate that ballots and not bullets would establish the Israeli government. Parties representing 111 out of 120 Knesset members recommended Peres as Rabin's successor.

Daniel 11:20 continued, Then shall stand up in his estate a
    raiser of taxes in the glory of the kingdom: but within
    *few days he shall be destroyed, neither in anger, nor in
    battle.*

Prime Minister Shimon Peres was only in office **a few days**, approximately 6 months. He succeeded Rabin in November 1995, and remained there until the new elections were held in May 1996. Peres was **destroyed, and it wasn't from anger nor battle**. He simply was voted out! His destruction was foretold in Daniel 5:25-28, "(v. 25) . . . MENE, MENE, TEKEL, UPHARSIN . . . (v. 26) MENE; God hath numbered thy kingdom, and finished it. (v. 27) TEKEL; Thou art weighed in the balances, and art found wanting. (v. 28) PERES; Thy kingdom is divided, and given to the Medes and Persians [the enemy]." Peres' *appointed* days are over. God has *finished* his kingdom. He is *found only wanting*, desiring a new Middle East, which by his hand shall never prosper. Peres *divided the kingdom* and gave it to the enemy. All in all, God allowed him to do so as part of His unfolding plan.

*It is common knowledge, among prophecy teachers, that this next verse is referring to the Antichrist. The *Revell Bible Dictionary* further credits this idea commenting, "The later chapters of Daniel are prophetic . . . . [C]hs. 11, 12 contain obscure prophecies of events associated with history's end" (20).

> Daniel 11:21, And in his estate shall stand up a vile person, to whom they ***shall not give the honour of the kingdom*** . . . .

To the surprise of everyone, Benjamin Netanyahu was elected to office on May 29, 1996. Charles W. Holmes, of Cox News Service noted, "Some critics view[ed] Netanyahu's election as a step back that could reignite the Palestinian 'intifada,' the violent uprising that faded after Israel and the PLO signed their landmark accord in 1993" (21). Netanyahu has been scrutinized as a hard-liner and a threat to the Middle East peace process. His victory is certainly not what the Clinton administration wanted since they had been nurturing the peace process from 1993. In fact, Lee Michael Katz wrote in *USA Today*, "Clinton all but endorsed Peres, and privately, Netanyahu aides say they were rebuffed in attempts to visit Clinton during one of Netanyahu's regular U.S. trips" (22). Along with Clinton, "Arab leaders [also] voted for Labor Prime Minister Shimon Peres. While realizing the possibility that their Israeli negotiating partner might lose, they apparently almost discounted it" (23). Feeling threatened by the Israeli election of conservative Benjamin Netanyahu, 21 Arab leaders gathered together for their first summit in six years. They did this in an attempt to urge Israel to prove its commitment to the peace process.

No one wanted to give Benjamin Netanyahu "the honour of the kingdom." Across the board, his election was a major upset to political world leaders. Benjamin Netanyahu defied everything the U.N. Resolution 242 called for. The Oslo Peace Accords of 1993 were drafted according to the U.N. Resolution 242 that requires Israel to return to her pre-1967 boundaries. This is where they developed the land for peace idea. Netanyahu claimed he would not trade land for peace. He said no to the releasing of the Golan Heights, East Jerusalem, and no to the control of the West Bank. The policy positions held by Benjamin Netanyahu were in direct opposition to the demands of other political world leaders. His recent decision to build 6,500 new homes in East Jerusalem has proven to be a prime example. Worldwide denunciation has come against Israel in making such a move: "Japanese Prime Minister Ryutaro Hashimoto called it a 'negative element' to the Middle East peace process . . . . Russia said it was 'ill-considered and untimely' . . . . The European Union, Britain and France condemned the decision when it was announced . . . . Iran's state radio called for international action, blasting the decision as an effort to 'Zionize' Jerusalem" (24).

> Daniel 11:21 continued, And in his estate shall stand up a *vile* person, to whom they shall not give the honor of the kingdom: *but he shall come in peaceably, and obtain the kingdom by flatteries*.

Benjamin Netanyahu is that *vile* person. His main concern is rising to the top, and he doesn't care how he gets there. An article titled, "Brash 'Bibi' Honed Political Skills Along American Lines," pointed out that "Netanyahu's rapid ascent from foreign diplomat to party chief has drawn sneers from critics who view him as more dedicated to his own success than to a Likud platform or right-wing ideology" (25). For example, when running against Shimon Peres, " . . . Mr. Netanyahu has tried to improve his position by an electoral alliance with Tsomet, a small hardline party controlled by a former army chief of staff, Rafael Eitan. Mr. Eitan withdrew from the race for the prime ministership . . . in return for a wedge of safe seats on the joint ticket" (26). Bibi's decision, to work with Mr. Eitan, a vowed secularist, sparked tension within his own party. Many times in Israel it is the religious vote which will win the election. Neither party, Likud nor Labor, could understand Netanyahu's reason for such a decision. *The Economist* reported "A joke heard in Knesset corridors suggests that if Mr. Netanyahu were to show as much flexibility in talks with the Palestinians as he did in haggling with Tsomet, Likud goals would be better served by leaving the talks in the hands of Mr. Peres" (27).

Even so, for a man who has never held a cabinet post, it was Bibi's use of illusionary words, containing **peace** and **flatteries**, which propelled him into office. Standing by more experienced contenders, Bibi appeared on a televised debate and proudly asked whom better than he could lead the Likud Party back into parliament. With flattering words Netanyahu claims,

> "**I am here . . . .** *I am the only one* **who can replace it . . . . I am the only one who can return Likud to government.**" Such arrogance drew snorts of contempt from his competitors, including a sniff from one that he was a "Napoleon" . . . "Bibi is unlike past Israeli politicians who stood for something," said a disapproving Labor government official. "But I have always said that we should not underestimate him" (28).

Known as a slick master of sound bites who doesn't always believe what he speaks, <u>Netanyahu has told the Israeli people what they have wanted to hear</u>. He has promised the Israelis peace with security without offering any further concessions to the Arabs. His campaign slogan read, "Netanyahu - we will bring peace and security."

Even *The New Republic* commented on his tactics:

> His followers readily concede he is aloof, ruthless . . . been caught cheating on his third wife. Still, they revere him: he is their hope for rallying the demoralized right for its final struggle over the territories . . . . Netanyahu tells Israelis they can have it all: security within and without. He promises to restore the élan of the Zionist past, when doing the impossible was considered routine . . . . For Israelis, the name "Netanyahu" symbolizes Zionism's defiance of the odds. (29)

In the delivery of his first post victory speech on Prime Time

TV, Netanyahu stated, "Tonight I extend the hand of peace to all Arab leaders and to our Palestinian neighbors . . . . We plan to advance the process of dialogue with all our neighbors in order to achieve stable peace, real peace, peace with security' . . . . A jubilant crowd chanted '**BIBI, *KING* OF ISRAEL**'" (30).

<u>Daniel 11:22</u>, **And with the arms of a flood shall they be overflown from before him, and shall be broken . . . .**

"And with the arms of a flood," what does a flood do? It comes in quickly and powerfully, pushing everything that's in its way out of its way. This is exactly what happened to the Israeli government. It was as if a flood came in and over night turned the Israeli government upside down. The election, to the world, was supposed to be a no-brainer. Everyone expected Shimon Peres to resume his position and for things to carry on as planned. He and his Labor Party were ahead of the Likud Party by 12-20 points. Knowing this, Shimon Peres decided to push up the elections from late October to May 28th. What a fatal mistake, for in February and March, a series of suicide bombings from militant Islamic groups helped alter the Jewish vote. Overnight, Israel's parliament was *"overflown,* **[wash away (31)]** *from before him."* Shockingly to everyone, Benjamin Netanyahu and his <u>new government</u> would now take office. The Liberal Labor would no longer be in control; under this pretense, both the Clinton Administration and the Arabs felt a little uneasy. "'*<u>We call on the new government</u>* to implement the principle of the exchange of land for peace,' said a statement of the PLO Executive Committee" (32).

The new election law made this election quite different from the previous ones. When it went into effect, the people were enabled to have a split ballot. In the past, voters could only vote for Parliament, but now they would be entitled to vote for both Prime Minister and Parliament. "One of the surprising consequences of the new election law was the <u>strong showing of small parties at the expense of the two major parties</u>," reported the *Tampa Tribune* (33). Wilbur Landrey also reported that
Labor and Likud together . . . lost 20 seats between them,

11 for Labor, now with only 33, and nine for Likud. Its 31 Knesset members will also henceforth include the freeloaders from special-interest groups Netanyahu wooed into Likud with promises of seats. The demanding religious bloc of parties have won big in winning 25 seats. So, in winning seven, has Natan Sharansky's Y'Israel B'Aliya of Immigrants from the former Soviet Union. A Third Way Party whose main plank is refusal to give up the Golan won four. (34)

Daniel 11:22 continued, And with the arms of a flood shall they be overflown from before him, **and shall be broken; yea, also the prince of the covenant.**

Along with the defeat of the government, the prince of the covenant was also broken. Israel's Prime Minister Shimon Peres, known as the **architect of the peace process** was also destroyed! The Jewish community wanted a change, and their voices were heard. The liberal Labor, having the majority in parliament, was pushed out from their position. Their leader Shimon Peres, the prince of the covenant, was pushed out along with them. A Times Wires article noted, "It is unclear whether Netanyahu's apparent victory means that most Israelis reject the policy of conceding land, or if they believe Peres moved too quickly, without sufficient guarantees for security" (35). In addition, on May 31, 1996, *The Tampa Tribune* reported, The "[p]reliminary breakdowns of the vote indicated Netanyahu led by 10 percentage points among Jewish voters and took 95 percent of the ultra-Orthodox religious vote. For his part, Peres received 95 percent of the votes of Israeli Arabs" (36).

The same *Tribune* article also explained that

For Peres, 72, a defeat in the election would mark a major personal blow. In 50 years at the pinnacle of Israeli politics, his innumerable achievements were marred by the fact that he led his party in three previous elections, and failed to win even once. Even before the final count was in, younger Labor ministers were maneuvering to succeed Peres. (37)

And Wilbur Landrey suggested, "Finally, barring that biblical miracle, Netanyahu is the big winner and Peres the big loser. Peres . . . seems to have stayed too long. A journalist who admires and has been close to him for years nevertheless said Thursday, expressing the brutal realism of Israeli politics: '**If he doesn't go voluntarily, they will throw him out**'" (38).

Daniel 11:23, And *after the league [to join (together) (39)] made with him* he shall work deceitfully . . . .

Why does the Word say, "**after**" the league "**made with him**" he shall work deceitfully? It's because the law gives Bibi 45 days to present his coalition to parliament. *If he fails to form his cabinet within the allotted time, new elections for prime minister could be held.* If he presents his coalition and it doesn't receive a majority vote in parliament, then new elections for both parliament and prime minister would occur. Therefore, Netanyahu, is not secure in his position until after the approval of his chosen cabinet. On June 18, 1996, the new 120-member Knesset endorsed Netanyahu's cabinet and swore him into office.

Daniel 11:23 continued, And after the league made with him *he shall work deceitfully* . . . .

Once, the "league" was made by him, Bibi began to *work deceitfully*. The people who voted for him did so on the pretense that things would change. Things were now going to take a different path! After all, he did make many "heart felt" promises to the Israelis, and surely he would keep most of them. Time tells all though, and actions speak louder than words. Bibi has already started to backslide on most of his claims; for example, "Netanyahu said during his campaign that he would not consider returning any of the Golan to Syria. [Yet, once in office], . . . Israel's new foreign minister said he would not rule out territorial compromise on the Golan Heights in exchange for peace with Syria" (40). Netanyahu was against the Israeli-Palestinian accords, but now he has changed his view to accept

Palestinian autonomy in the West Bank and Gaza. He says he will continue peace talks.

Two other particular claims shine the light on his darkness. One such claim he made was on February 5, 1996: "'I will not meet with Yasser Arafat'" (41). On September 4, 1996, less than three months into office, Benjamin Netanyahu met with the Palestinian President. This meeting ". . . was noteworthy because it was the first time the leader of Israel's right wing sat down with the founder of the Palestine Liberation Organization, a man it has reviled for decades as a terrorist" (42). Outraged by Netanyahu's actions,

> Amid shouts of "traitor!" and "resign!" from Likud Party activists stunned by Wednesday's meeting and handshake with the Palestinian leader, . . . [a] vocal minority of Likud stalwarts, especially Jewish settlers and religious nationalists, considered the meeting a **betrayal** of their dream of holding onto the West Bank and Gaza, where the Palestinians want to turn autonomy into a state . . . . "**Bibi has betrayed us!**" said Amram Cohavi, a veteran Likud member . . . . In an interview with Israel TV, Netanyahu said he would fire Cabinet ministers who oppose him: "Ministers who do not sit comfortably with (the Arafat meeting) will not be in the government." (43)

Furthermore, Bibi vowed to never withdraw troops from Hebron. This particular promise was extremely important to the Jewish people. Hebron is holy unto them. It carries major biblical significance, to name just a few: (A) Abraham first pitched his tent there and built an altar unto the Lord; (B) Abraham and his family were buried there; (C) God gave this land to Caleb as an "inheritance"; (D) David was anointed king there. On January 15, 1997, Bibi defected on his commitment to stay in Hebron and also agreed within two years to withdraw from important parts of the occupied West Bank. This was quite a shock to the Israelis mainly because this land was considered "'Eretz Israel', the land God promised them in biblical times . . . Even though Israeli Prime Minister Benjamin Netanyahu will never admit it publicly, that is effectively what he is doing -

trading away major parts of Eretz Israel and with them the biblical promise" (44).

The confirming of the peace treaty caused a major ruckus when Bibi presented the objective before his bitterly divided cabinet. "After 12 hours of rancorous debate, the pact was approved - but only after Netanyahu was vilified by far-right opponents. In Hebron, a bus carried a banner that read: 'Bibi is a traitor,'" reported the *St. Petersburg Times* (45). Crowds of angry people walked the streets carrying banners, which demoralized the name of Israel's Prime Minister.

If what you've read has not been enough to convince you of his **"deceitful acts"** since taking office, then consider this: In fifty years of independence, never before has Israel ever had a Prime Minister up for indictment charges: "Benjamin Netanyahu . . . had been accused by police of committing a *'breach of trust'*, an oddity of Israeli criminal law that applies when a government official *doesn't carry out his public duties for the benefit of the nation*" (46). In one of the biggest scandals ever, the Prime Minister appointed Roni Bar-On, a little-known criminal lawyer as attorney general. A wave of protest arose among the country's legal establishment because Bar-On was viewed as unqualified for the position. Bar-On resigned in less than one day in office.

"On Jan. 22, [1997,] Israel's Channel 1 news reported that Aryeh Deri, leader of the ultra-Orthodox Shas Party, traded his party's support for the Hebron deal for the Bar-On appointment," according to the article "Police Seek Netanyahu Indictment" (47). Once in office, Bar-On was supposed to keep Deri, a popular leader among "religious" Israelis, out of jail. The article also indicated that "Deri has been on trial for three years for corruption stemming from his term as interior minister" (48). Prosecutors stated, despite the prime minister's actions being puzzling, they lacked the evidence needed to try him: "'The decision is too close - for lack of sufficient evidence - the case against the prime minister . . . . From the evidence there is suspicion that there were other (than legitimate) considerations. [B]ut we don't think this can be proved beyond a reasonable doubt'" (49).

<u>Daniel 11:23 continued</u>, And after the league made with him he shall work deceitfully: *for he shall come up, and shall become strong with a small people.*

After this latest scandal, the peace process has been expected to slow down: "David Bar Illan, the prime minister's senior adviser, admitted little, if any, progress could be expected in the next two months" (50). The *St. Petersburg Times* reported that within Netanyahu's own coalition, the fire raged:

> The leader of the Third Way, a centrist party in the ruling coalition, said whether or not charges are filed, Netanyahu may have to resign to restore the government's tainted image. "If it becomes clear there are serious improprieties as far as democracy and the public are concerned, we won't be able to support the government and will call for early elections," Yehuda Harel said. [Other members of Netanyahu's cabinet were wavering also.] Natan Sharanksy's Immigrants Party, which controls seven seats and has broad influence in the Russian immigrant community, called a meeting to decide whether to support the prime minister. The issue is "not only a political crisis," legislator Marina Slobotkin said. "<u>It's a moral crisis</u>." (51)

Benjamin Netanyahu's deceitful act surely abased him but not for long. The Bible says he shall not only *come up* with small people, but he shall also *become strong with small people.* Prior to this latest happening, it was believed that

> Netanyahu's Likud Party would form a broad-based coalition with Shimon Peres' pro-peace Labor Party, which it defeated a year ago. The idea was that if Likud and Labor got together, they could form a government excluding the hard-line rightist and religious parties that refuse to even think [about] trading Israeli-occupied land for peace with Palestinians, especially when that land is in Jerusalem. But the corruption allegations against Netanyahu, even without a formal indictment, make a Labor-Likud coalition government almost impossible no

matter how beneficial it might be to the peace process. Now Peres is calling for Netanyahu's immediate resignation and agitating for new elections. That effort is unlikely to succeed and in any case, Peres is stepping down as Labor leader in June [Peres is finished]. (52)

At any rate, if Netanyahu did have any thoughts of uniting with the Labor Party, he will now be forced to stay with the "smaller parties" that he reached out to ten months ago. In fulfillment of Bible prophecy, "he shall come up, *and* shall become strong with small people."

> Daniel 11:24, *He shall enter peaceably even upon the fattest places of the province* . . . .

The word 'province' in Hebrew means region (53). "[F]at places in Hebrew literally means '**of the oils of the land!**'" according to Victor Mordecai, author of *Is Fanatic Islam a Global Threat?* (54). In the *Middle East region,* the Arabs occupy the *oils of the land.* Benjamin Netanyahu has definitely **entered peaceably** among his Arab neighbors. He has had negotiations with Palestinian leader Yasser Arafat, Jordan's King Hussein and Egyptian President Hosni Mubarak. When meeting with Mubarak, "Netanyahu said he was ready to renew talks with Syria 'right away' . . ." (55). Netanyahu, in his first meeting with U.S. Secretary of State Warren Christopher stated, "'There will be no shortage of communications channels, and we'll broaden the communications'" (56). After his deal on Hebron, Netanyahu stated, "' . . . we shall move on to the principal task before us, and that is the negotiations on the final status arrangements'" (57).

> Daniel 11:24 continued, He shall enter peaceably even upon the fattest places of the province; and *he shall do that which his fathers have not done, nor his fathers' fathers* . . . .

What have the Jewish people dreamed about for the last 2,000 years? They have dreamed about their temple and establishing a throne of authority where the King would rule and reign from forever. In his Israeli guidelines, Benjamin Netanyahu, unlike the Prime Ministers before him, plans for "Zionist fulfillment." His election was thought of by many Jews as an act of God, and was it ever. Benjamin Netanyahu will accomplish what his fathers' fathers have not done. He is going to give the Jews their strongest desire. He has claimed he will establish the throne of David for them! Listen to how he addresses the Knesset on June 18, 1996:

> "I was fortunate to be the *first* among Israeli Prime Ministers to be born [Oct. 21, 1949] after the establishment of the State of Israel. The torch has been passed unto us by the generation born with the founding of the state of Israel 1948. We want a stable and lasting peace, not a temporary one. A fleeting agreement, such a peace is based first of all on the security of Israel and its citizens. The test of peace agreements is security and on this we shall not compromise. But, above all, we will guard and strengthen Jerusalem, the eternal capital of the Jewish people, undivided under the sovereignty of the State of Israel. During the term of this Knesset, we will mark the fiftieth Independence Day of the State of Israel in the beginning of the twenty-first century. *We've reached the days, generations of Jews have hoped for and prayed for; the Jewish dream has been realized. In us, the words of the Prophet Amos have been fulfilled. I SHALL ESTABLISH FOR THEM DAVID'S FALLEN TABERNACLE AND IT WILL WITH HIS HELP STAND FOR EVER AND EVER."* (58)

The General Superintendent of the U.P.C., Nathaniel A. Urshan commented:

> . . . the Likud party with other conservative parties has gained the majority of seats in the Knesset . . . . This means that the strong Orthodox leanings has the upper hand in much of what will take place in the future politically. It also means that the Temple Mount Faithful may have backing for the projects they desire to put into action. One project is to rebuild the Temple of Solomon

40

on Mount Moriah . . . . I doubt very much that Prime Minister Netanyahu will hold back the Temple Mount Faithful but rather give them the opportunity to fulfill the desire of this project. The Temple Mount Faithful is led militarily by a man named Gershon Salomon. He has promised to rebuild the Temple by the year 2000 on Mount Moriah . . . . If this comes to pass, look for a terrible war in Israel. And then stop and consider the possibilities of this escalating into a future Armageddon. (59)

In the Old Testament, the priest, before entering the temple area or Jerusalem's temple, must first be purified. According to Mosaic Law, if any of them had been rendered impure by contact with a dead body they had to be cleansed. In Numbers 19, the ashes of a red heifer, of her third year, mixed with water were used to accomplish this task. It has been said Melody, the first red heifer to be miraculously born in Northern Israel since 70 A.D., could be ready to be sacrificed around the year 1999. "Avraham Poraz, a member of Parliament from the leftist Meretz Party said, 'That cow represents the risk of a massive religious war . . .'" (60). But whether or not it is Melody or any other red heifer, the point is war is ready to be raged in Israel.

Daniel 11:27, *And both these kings' hearts shall be to do mischief, and they shall speak lies at one table; but it shall not prosper: `for yet the end shall be at the time appointed*.

The Lord spoke to me as I was reading here and said, "Just like Judas did to me; he is going to sell out his country." Bibi, like Judas, is going to sit at a table and betray his own country, but the transgression will not prosper, for the end will be at the time appointed. Judas' past is the key to the Antichrist's future. Understand that Judas betrayed Christ times two, first at Bethany then at the *table*.

First of all, when Jesus was at Bethany, Mary poured some very costly ointment on Christ's feet. Judas, murmuring, wanted to know why the ointment wasn't sold and given to the poor: "This he said, not that he cared for the poor; but because he was

41

a thief" (John 12:6). Jesus stated, in Mark 14, the woman came to anoint His body for the burying. Judas didn't want to hear this. He wanted his earthly reward now. So, Judas gave up on the idea of an *earthly kingdom restored to Israel*, and he went to the chief priest to betray Christ for thirty pieces of silver, *the price of sheep for the slaughter.* He made a covenant to deliver Jesus to the opposition at the "opportune time." The story of the Antichrist is a replica of Judas' day. Benjamin Netanyahu made a deal with the enemy and *sold out the birthright, the Jews inherited land of Israel*; this marked the first betrayal. As Judas did with Christ, Benjamin dealt with the Israeli's inheritance thereby *setting the sheep up for the slaughter.*

Later, Judas with his "*heart*" now being evil sat at a "*table*" and betrayed Christ for a *second time. This time he sold out the cause*, and this was the final thrust. (The "cause" will be discussed momentarily.) The Bible says when Judas left the table he went into the "night." Judas, with this last action, chose whose side he was on. There would be no hope for him now and Matthew 27:3 confirms this stating, "he saw that he was condemned." It was too late for Judas; his deal never prospered. In his second betrayal, Benjamin Netanyahu with his heart now being evil shall sit at a table and *sell out the cause*. Like Daniel 11:27 states, ". . . but it *shall not prosper*: for yet the end shall be at the time appointed." (*Verse 28 confirms a deal was made in verse 27.)

> Daniel 11:28, *Then* **shall he return into his land with** *great riches*; [thus, he made an agreement] **and his heart shall be against the "holy" covenant**; and he shall do *exploits*, and return to his own land.

Notice how the covenant is referred to as the "**holy covenant**" in this verse. Before, in verse 22, it was only called the **covenant**. Why the name change? To help explain what had transpired between verses 22 and 28, we need to understand something about the **anointed one**. Old Testament prophets foretold that the Messiah, "anointed one," would appear *to set the captive free* and *reclaim the throne of David* (Isa. 61:1, Ps.

42

2:2-9). The throne of David was located on the most sacred site in all of Jerusalem, Mount Moriah, also known as Mount Zion. In brief, God promised Israel a "*house*" that shall not be moved (II Sam. 7:6-16). David wanted to build the house, but Solomon his son was appointed of the Lord to build it instead. Thus, Solomon built the temple on Mt. Moriah the threshingplace where David had also sacrificed, II Chron. 3:1. The Ark of the Covenant where the Lord was "enthroned" was moved from the city of David, Mt. Zion, to Mt. Moriah, and the staves for the first time were removed from the ark symbolizing an establishment of authority. Mt. Moriah would then become known as Mt. Zion the place where our King would rule from forever. The *Revell Bible Dictionary* states, "After Solomon built the Jerusalem Temple on a site north of the citadel, the name Zion was extended to incorporate the Temple Mount . . . . The name continued to be extended, becoming a metaphor for all Jerusalem as the religious capital of Israel, and later as a metaphor for Israel and all its inhabitants" (61).

David, the king of Israel, was a great warrior; the Jews expected the one who would take David's throne, or place of authority, to be even mightier. They wanted out from under the Roman rule. The Israelis had been waiting for their earthly kingdom to be restored unto Israel. Because of Jesus Christ's lowliness, the Jews rejected Him as the "anointed one," who would fulfill the prophecies. Therefore, the Jews are still looking for their Messiah to reclaim the throne of David. So when Benjamin Netanyahu stands in the holy place, "Mt. Zion," and claims to be Israel's King, the Jews being blind to his identity will bless him as the anointed one, their Messiah.

Now recall the "covenant" in Da. 11:22 dealt only with the birthright (refer to verse 22 on pgs. 33-35). Yet in verse 28 the covenant is referred to as the "holy covenant." You see, between verses 22 and 28 it has been said that a throne of authority shall be established in line 24 and that Netanyahu shall claim to be God. Netanyahu will not only step in as king but also as high priest to Israel. Thereby, here is something *even more significant* to consider. Netanyahu claiming to be the "High Priest," the prophesied anointed one who would reunite mankind to God, will be against what Christ came to do. The devil does not want the captive to be set free and will be against the reunion.

The Antichrist with his heart against the *holy* covenant, against man's reunion with God, will mimic Judas Iscariot. When Judas sat at the table with Jesus Christ, he did more than just betray our Lord and Master. ***Judas betrayed the "cause," and Netanyahu will do the same.*** Unlike Judas, Netanyahu will not sit at the table with Jesus; yet, he will sit at the table to betray the cause. *Understand the cause is not the death, burial and resurrection, even though that is necessary to get to God, but ***THE CAUSE IS GOD BRINGING MAN BACK INTO HIS HOLY PRESENCE*** *(see also I Tim. 1:15, 16).*

Allow me to explain:

Adam and Eve's transgression in the Garden of Eden caused a wide chasm, which separated man from God. Jesus Christ, or the *"anointed one"* is the *". . . one mediator between **God** and **men**"* (I Timothy 2:5). He is the only one capable of bridging the gap. The gospel, the death, burial, and resurrection, is the solution to the problem, and it is most definitely necessary. Yet once the **cause** is accomplished, **God reuniting Himself to man**, then Sonship will cease.

I Corinthians 15:24-28 states,

> (v. 24) Then cometh the end, *when he shall have delivered up the kingdom* to God, even the Father [the Son is delivering the kingdom back to the Father]; when he shall have put down all rule and all authority and power. (v. 25) For he must reign, **till** he hath put all enemies under his feet. (v. 26) The last enemy that shall be destroyed is death. (v. 27) For he hath put all things under his feet. But when he saith all things are put under him, it is manifest that he is excepted, which did put all things under him. (v. 28) And when all things shall be subdued unto him, then shall the Son also himself be subject unto him that put all things under him, that God may be all in all.

Many people do not understand that this is speaking of offices and not people. *Once the kingdom is delivered up to God and death is destroyed then there will no longer be a need for a *redeemer*, for "the office of the Sonship (mediator, intercessor) will end and He will be known not as Son, but as the Almighty God, and God will be all in all" (62). <u>Nevertheless, Benjamin Netanyahu will sell out the cause. He, like Judas sitting at the table, will sell out to what our Lord wants *the most*, which is you and I getting back to God</u>!

> <u>Daniel 11:30</u>, **For the ships of Chittim [Cyprus (63)] shall come against him: therefore he shall be grieved, and return [retreat, lodge (64)]. . . .**

The Island of Cypress is located in the Mediterranean, sixty miles off the coast of Syria. Cypress contains two types of people, the Turks and the Greeks. The island of Cypress shall come against Netanyahu and push him into keeping his previous promise of betrayal held at a table. Feeling the pressure to *hand over*, Bibi shall be grieved, and return (to *lodge*) thinking to himself.

> <u>Daniel 11:30 continued</u>, For the ships of Chittim [Cypress] shall come against him: therefore he shall be grieved, and return, **and have indignation against the holy covenant: so shall he do; he shall even *return*, and have intelligence with them that forsake [relinquish (65)] the holy covenant.**

Being now possessed of Satan, the Antichrist will follow in the same planned course of events as Judas. What did Christ say to Judas, "**THAT THOU DOEST, DO QUICKLY**" (John 13:27). Judas then leaves the table to ***RETURN*** <u>with a multitude of Jewish people, i.e., chief priests, elders and Pharisees</u>. They having in mind to destroy the "*temple of God*," or Jesus Christ, then lead Christ into the power of the Roman hands. Benjamin Netanyahu shall follow in Judas' footsteps. Daniel 11:30 states concerning the Antichrist, "**SO SHALL HE DO.**" Netanyahu, against mankind's reunion with God, will ***RETURN*** <u>and have intelligence with them (Jewish leaders)</u> that forsake the holy covenant. They are going to desecrate the *temple of God* as shown in the next verse, (see also II Th. 2:4). It's the kiss of death! He is going to betray his country with the kiss of death!

> Daniel 11:31, **And arms [as with Judas, power] shall stand on his part, and they shall pollute the sanctuary of strength, and shall take away the daily sacrifice, and they shall place the abomination that maketh desolate**.

Notice in Da. 11:31 *"arms"* shall stand on Netanyahu's part to desecrate the temple of God. The Antichrist's power will ultimately come from the men in the region of the former Eastern Roman Empire. The men in the east will, as in Judas' day, desecrate the temple of God. A greater description is given on pgs. 57-58.

> Daniel 11:32, **And such as do wickedly against the covenant shall he corrupt by flatteries:** but the people that do know their God shall be strong, and do exploits.

It is important to note the covenant in this verse is no longer referred to as holy like in verses 28 and 30. The abomination of desolation has taken place. Netanyahu has sat in the temple of God showing himself to be God. The transgression has come to its fullest as the Israeli leader through deception will try to take away mankind's hope in reuniting to our Lord. Thus, he will have betrayed the cause.

> Daniel 11:32 continued, And such as do wickedly against the covenant shall he corrupt by flatteries: **but the people that do know their God shall be strong, and do exploits**.

Do the Jews **know** God? Do those that haven't taken on His name in baptism **know** God? Who **knows** God? We do, the church. We know Jesus Christ. We have been baptized in His name and filled with His Spirit. We, who know God and have obeyed the gospel of Jesus Christ, shall be strong doing exploits. Hallelujah! II Thess. 1:7-10 attests to this:

> (v. 7) And to you who are troubled rest with us, when the Lord Jesus shall be revealed from heaven with his mighty angels, (v. 8) In flaming fire taking vengeance on them that ___know___ ___not___ ___God,___ **and** *that __obey not the gospel__ of our* ***Lord Jesus Christ***: (v. 9) Who shall be punished with everlasting destruction from the presence of the Lord, and from the glory of his power; (v. 10) *When he shall come to be glorified in his saints*, and to be admired in all them that believe (because *our testimony* among you was believed) *__in that day__*.

Brother and Dr. Larry Smith, author of *Rightly Dividing the Word* commented:

> Notice how he [Paul] mentions the gospel he preached as being the same gospel that will judge people at the coming of the Lord. Verse 10: *Because our testimony was believed, meaning they believed what the apostles preached (66).

II Thess. 1:7-10 proves that the message the apostles preached will not change until Jesus Christ comes for His church. Galatians 1:8 states, "But though we, or an angel from heaven, preach any other gospel unto you than that which we have preached unto you, let him be accursed." God felt so strongly about this statement that Paul reiterated it again in verse 9. Those people, whatever nationality they are who are preaching the death, burial and resurrection of Jesus Christ, shall be witnessing in that day.

Chapter 4
Son of Perdition

One day while I was traveling on the interstate, the Lord opened my understanding to the story of Judas. He showed me that Judas was the key to understanding endtime prophecy concerning the reign of the Antichrist. I instantly saw a flash of a temple in my mind, and I knew immediately God was *comparing the temple to Himself.* In John 2:19, Jesus stated, **"DESTROY THIS TEMPLE**, and in three days I will raise it up."** Jesus Christ called Himself *a temple*, and He was the temple of God. ***Judas sold out Jesus, and the type and shadow of this is the Antichrist will sell out their "temple*."** Once the story of Judas' life has been explored, you will have a greater understanding of the future events that are about to occur.

Studying the story, we first notice that Judas was a Jew. He was not just any Jew; he was a greedy Jewish thief who held a position as the treasurer. Jesus Himself had handpicked Judas to follow Him and gave him control over the moneys that supplied their needs. Certainly Judas, with such a prominent position, would never betray Jesus or His followers. He appeared to be their friend. The apostles had no idea he would betray them, yet Jesus, *sitting at a table* with His apostles said, "one of you shall betray me" (John 13:21). Entered by Satan, Judas had already gone to the chief priests and captains to betray Jesus. He had made a covenant with them and promised to deliver Jesus for money, thirty pieces of silver. Likewise, the Prime Minister of Israel "holds the bag." At the head of the table, he will represent all power and authority. His country, like the apostles, will trust in him to meet their needs, especially financial ones. The Jewish people will not even see the betrayal coming. Who would expect their leader to betray one's own country? Under the influence of Satan, he too will *sit at a table* and his *heart*, like Judas', will be to do mischief. He, too, will promise to turn over the temple at the opportune time. Daniel 11:27, 28 informs us of this: "(v. 27) And both these kings' *hearts* shall be to do mischief, and they shall speak lies at one *table* [he strikes a *deal* turning over the temple]; *but it shall not prosper* [as with Judas, it won't pay off]: for yet the end shall be at the time appointed. [Note: the next line confirms a deal was made.] (v. 28) *Then shall he return into his land with great riches.*"

The Israelis will believe Netanyahu is acting in their own best interest. They will not understand what is taking place. Remember Peter wanted to know who the betrayer was, and Jesus replied, "He it is, to whom I shall give a sop, when I have dipped it" (John 13:26). He then dipped the sop, gave it to Judas, and said, "That thou doest, do quickly" (John 13:27).

That thou doest, do quickly. These are powerful words, for Judas, now having received the sop from Jesus, immediately *left the table* and went *into the night*. Judas had crossed over the line to receive power from the darkness that is from Satan. Recall Da. 11:30 pgs. 45-46 Judas Iscariot *returned as the "guide"* to a band of people. This multitude that followed Judas felt they needed to carry swords and staves in order to take Jesus Christ, the temple of God.

The following verses will illustrate Judas' past being performed once again in the future. Remember Daniel 11 is futuristic. Daniel 11:30-31 explains the situation:

> . . . (v. 30) therefore he [the Antichrist] shall be grieved, and return [or **turn away** (1)], and have indignation against the holy covenant: **so shall he do** [what did Jesus say to Judas, "That thou doest, do quickly"]; he shall even **return** [like Judas with the <u>Jews</u>], and have <u>intelligence</u> with them that forsake the holy covenant. (v. 31) And <u>arms</u> [<u>Roman power</u>] shall stand on his part, and they shall pollute the sanctuary of strength [meaning the temple, which is symbolic for Jesus Christ], and shall take away the daily sacrifice.

In II Thessalonians, the Antichrist sits in the **temple of God** claiming to be God. The Antichrist, like Judas, will be the "**guide**" to them that take the temple of God. This is history repeating itself.

Luke, in Acts 1:16 confirms the above:

> Men and brethren, this scripture must needs have been fulfilled, which the Holy Ghost by the *mouth of David*

spake before concerning Judas, which was *guide to them that took Jesus*.

Acts 1:16 here refers us to the Psalm of David 109:6-8, which speaks of Judas:

Set thou a wicked man over him: and let Satan stand at his right hand [or be his power] . . . let him be condemned . . . Let his days be few; and *let another take his office* [or have the charge (2)].

"*Let another take his office*," these are strong, very meaningful words, and there are a couple of ways to interpret what is meant here. Acts 1:16, refers to the Psalm of David, that states, "*Let another take his office*," and *ties it together* with the fact that Judas *was "guide"* to them that took Jesus, the temple of God.

Judas was the *guide*. *Jesus was the temple of God*. Another will take Judas' office, the Antichrist, as the guide of an army that will desecrate the temple of God (II Thess. 2:4, Da. 11:31). Like Judas, he will "*have the charge*" over a multitude of people, and with him as their leader they will take the temple of God. Some of you might say, "Well, another taking his office refers to Mathias taking over his apostleship." This is true. However, God's Word is not simplistic; it is revelatory. There is usually always a deeper meaning than what may be our initial understanding. Judas was a *betrayer*, and he played two roles! To one he was an apostle, and to the other he was a guide.

Judas was titled the son of perdition. **There is only one other person in the whole entire Bible with this same title, and that is the Antichrist**. Think about that! Every word God speaks is for a reason. These two men have the same title, and this is powerful! Why does the Word of God call both of these men the son of perdition? *It is because Judas' past is the key to the Antichrist's future*! The Antichrist is going to take Judas' office as the son of perdition. Look at II Thessalonians chapter 2 again. The church is inquiring about the coming of Christ, the beginning of their eternal life. Paul, in verses 3, 4, 6 and 7, answers them. Verse 3 states, "Let no man deceive you by any means: for that day shall not come, *except* there come a falling away first, and that man of sin be revealed, the son of perdition."

The "son of perdition" must be revealed, and God is revealing him right now!

Verse 4 continues on now describing the son of perdition; it states, "Who opposeth and exalteth himself above all that is called God, or that is worshipped; so that he **as God** sitteth in the temple of God, shewing himself that he is God." In verse 4, the Antichrist sits in the temple as God. What was God? He was a *Jew* who was 100% human and 100% deity. He was God man, God in a man, Spirit in flesh. The *mystery of Godliness is God in flesh, thus Jesus Christ, the Son of God* (see I Timothy 3:16). Satan always tries to mimic God. Remember that the Antichrist sits in the temple *as God,* a spirit in a man, a Jewish man. This explains the *mystery of iniquity, or Satan in flesh, thus the Antichrist, the son of perdition.*

Verse 6 states, "And **now** ye know what withholdeth that he [the Antichrist] might be revealed in his time." Paul was saying here *now*, right now without any more explanation, you should know what is keeping us from eternal life; the son of perdition must be revealed. The Antichrist being revealed is the topic in the above. Paul now is going to expound more on this in verse 7: "**FOR the mystery of iniquity doth *already* work**." In other words, this is nothing new. The son of perdition, the Antichrist whom he is talking about, is nothing new. Satan entered Judas, who also was called the son of perdition. God strategically placed the title son of perdition in this particular chapter to show us something. The Lord purposely used the word *mystery of iniquity* in verse 7, along with other words that either allude to or mean possession (recall pgs.15-16 at this point).

The *Revell Bible Dictionary* states, "Judas, called the 'son of perdition' in Jn. 17:12 (KJV), is described as 'the one doomed to [eternal] destruction,' a **term otherwise reserved for the Antichrist and his followers** (2 Th. 2:3; Rev. 17:8, 11)" (3). We have discussed II Thessalonians 2:3; now let us look at Revelation 17:8, 11. Revelation 17:8 reads, "The beast that thou sawest <u>was</u>, and <u>is not</u>; and shall ascend out of the bottomless pit, and go into perdition: and they that dwell on the earth shall wonder . . . when they behold the beast that **was**, and **is not**, and **yet is**." The beast that **was**, and **is not**, and **yet is**, has been around **long before** Judas and his followers: it "**was**" in heaven, (discussed in ch. 10). However, Judas and his men were only tools or instruments that Satan used for a period of time. A type of the past will be repeated or represented once again in the future. *The Antichrist **is not** Judas; he **yet is** in the sense that they have the **same planned course of events.** Remember II Thes. 2:7 states, ". . . only he [Satan] who now letteth [keep in memory (4)] will let [or possess (5)], until he be taken out of the way." Satan is keeping his plan in memory; the Antichrist and his followers are the continuation of it.

Scripture substantiates that when demons are on the earth, they seek bodies to live in: "The legion of demons which Jesus cast into a herd of pigs had begged him not to send them back to the 'Abyss' (Lk. 8:31)" (6). Thus, these evil spirits or evil forces, which live in the Abyss, a mysterious realm of the dead, shall "*ascend*," meaning they will *arise* and go *in* the followers of the Antichrist. The Greek definitions of the words 'ascend' and 'bottomless' used in Revelation 17:8 support what has been said:

A) Ascend - meaning to *arise*, is also linked to the words *in*, through, *repetition* (7) (something repeated (8)).

B) Bottomless - means *abyss* (9), which stands for a mysterious realm of the dead (10).

Again it is all a repeating of the past. Judas and his followers represented the beast that "**was**"; it was in heaven. Yet, it is the beast that "**is not**" because it is not the same people being used to bring about Satan's plan. Nevertheless, it's the beast that "**yet is**" because when it possesses these people and takes its position, "it" will live again.

Look closer at Revelation 17:8: "The beast that thou sawest was, and is not; and shall ascend out of the bottomless pit, and go into perdition: and they that dwell on the earth shall wonder . . . when they behold the beast that **was**, and **is not**, and *yet is*." **Notice the beast is only described as the **was** and **is not**, the words "*yet is*" *is absent until **after*** these spirits arise and possess or seize their positions. Then *after* the beast ascends, possessing the bodies it needs, it's described as the was, is not, "**and**" *yet is*.

In Revelation 17:7, 8, the beast spoken of is slightly different

53

from the beast in Revelation 17:10, 11. The difference is in their existence. The beast or the Antichrist's followers, in Revelation 17:7, 8, will ascend out of the bottomless pit; yet the beast or the Antichrist himself, mentioned in Revelation 17:10, 11, will arise to power after Satan is cast to this earth to enter into him (note page 17 and pg. 124). Then they shall unite to become one.

It was stated earlier that Benjamin Netanyahu, the "*son of perdition*," would take Judas' office; he will be the leader or the "**_GUIDE_**" to this beast. Revelation 17:12 states, "And the ten horns which thou sawest are ten kings, which have received no kingdom as yet; but receive power as kings one hour with the beast." They are going to unite, and Benjamin will be their *guide*. Possessed by Satan, the Antichrist, with his men, will have "*one hour*" of power. Interestingly enough, Luke 22:53 states the same thing concerning Judas and his followers: ". . . but this is your **hour**, and the **power of darkness**." *These men have the same planned course of events!* In both of these cases, Satan, through Judas and the Antichrist, is given "**one hour**" of power.

Power is given to Satan to have dominion over the saints for "one hour" just as he had with Christ. Daniel 7:25-27 emphasizes this:

> (v. 25) And he shall speak great words against the **most High**, and shall wear out the **saints of the most High**, and think to change times and laws: and they shall be given into his hand until a time and times and the dividing of time. (v. 26) But the judgment shall sit, and they shall take away his **dominion**, to consume and to destroy it unto the end. (v. 27) And the kingdom and dominion, and the greatness of the kingdom under the whole heaven, shall be given to the people of the saints of the most High, whose kingdom is an everlasting kingdom, and all dominions shall serve and obey him.

Christ said in John 15:20, "The servant is not greater than his lord. If they [the son of perdition with his evil alliances, as well as the world,] have persecuted me, they will also persecute you." Because of Jesus Christ's death, we now have life. The first church suffered with persecution; yet through their persecution came the growth of the church. *Search for Truth Bible Study* states,

> . . . [t]his part is undesirable. But it could be the motivating force that encourages the Church to finish its task. Jesus' words could apply to no other generation than ours. "Then shall they deliver you up to be afflicted, and shall kill you: and ye shall be hated of all nations for my name's sake" (Matthew 24:9). Persecution and hatred could be responsible for the final thrust: "And this gospel of the kingdom shall be preached in all the world for a witness unto all nations; and then shall the end come" (Matthew 24:14). (11)

Romans 8:38, 39 states, "(v. 38) For I am persuaded, that neither **death**, nor life, nor angels, nor principalities, nor powers, nor things present, **nor things to come** . . . (v. 39) shall be able to separate us from the love of God." I Thessalonians chapter 3 tells us we are **appointed** unto afflictions; verse 4 states, " . . . we told you before that we should suffer tribulation."

Understand that the great tribulation *is not* God's wrath; it is Satan's wrath. The word "great" is added because there will be more of it going on. Satan's wrath, mentioned in Revelation 12:12, is discussed on pages 16-23. When Judas and his men were approaching, it was Satan's hour of power. Christ was exceedingly sorrowful thinking of the time of evil that would come upon him. Yet, He said, ". . . nevertheless not my will, but thine, be done" (Luke 22:42). We need to understand God's will, and then align ourselves with it. The Word states, "And fear not them which kill the body, but are not able to kill the soul: but rather fear him which is able to destroy both soul and body in hell" (Matthew 10:28).

Once again, Judas' story matches perfectly in foreshadowing the reign of the Antichrist, even right down to the beast's "**hour of power**." To expound on *"their hour"* and the power of darkness, look at those who followed Judas, and compare them with the ten kings that will also follow the Antichrist. The men that followed Judas should be a type and a shadow of the ten kings mentioned in Revelation 17:12. They should be from the same region. Enlightenment comes concerning the ten horns or ten kings when we cross-reference Revelation 17:12 with Daniel chapter 2.

In Daniel chapter 2, Nebuchadnezzar, the king of Babylon, had a troublesome dream of which the Prophet Daniel gave the interpretation thereof. In his dream, the king had seen an image of a man. The man's body parts made of different metals represented five world empires: the head of gold, Babylon; the silver chest and arms, Medo-Persian; the brass stomach and thighs, Greece; the iron unified upper legs, Old Roman Empire. These four world empires are of the past. However, the image's feet or "ten toes" made of iron and clay represented a future evil kingdom, which will try to rule and reign prior to the return of Jesus Christ.

The ten toes are symbolic for the ten kings, which will have an "hour of power" with the Antichrist in Revelation 17:12. In proving the ten kings are from the same region as those that followed Judas, study the following. The feet and ten toes of Nebuchadnezzar's image consisted of two materials *IRON* and *CLAY*. Daniel 2:41-43 states,

> (v. 41) And whereas thou sawest the feet and toes, **part of potters' clay**, and **part of iron**, the kingdom shall be divided; but there shall be in it of the strength of the iron, forasmuch as thou sawest the iron mixed with miry clay. (v. 42) And as the *toes* of the feet were part of iron, and part of clay, so the kingdom shall be partly strong, and partly broken. (v. 43) And whereas thou sawest iron mixed with **miry clay** . . . but they shall not cleave one to another, even as iron is not mixed with clay.

First, let's study the substance clay, which is used in building this evil kingdom. God has placed descriptive words, such as, part and potters,' with the term clay to help reveal whom the clay is to us. Who is the potter, and who is the clay? Isaiah 64:8 reads, "O LORD, thou art our father; we are the clay, and thou our potter." Jesus is the potter and Israel is the clay. This becomes evident in Jeremiah chapter 18 when God compares Himself to the potter and Israel to the clay. Moreover, the Word says "part" potter's clay. Israel, even though she has been blinded, is still "part" of the clay; for the Bible says that God has

not cast away His people. In Judas' days, the chief priests, along with the more so called "respected" Jews, turned over Jesus Christ, the temple of God, into the Romans' hands. Therefore, **part** of the clay was evil.

Another clue given, concerning this world empire, is the word *miry* used to describe the clay. Now pay close attention. In the Hebrew, *miry* means *mud* (12). In Genesis 28:13-14, Jacob is promised the Abrahamic Covenant. God tells Jacob in verses 13 and 14, ". . . (v. 13) the *land whereon thou liest*, to thee will I give it, and to thy seed; (v. 14) And thy *seed* shall be as the *dust*." God compared Jacob's seed, Israel, who possesses the Promised Land, to the dust. *Dust* in this particular verse means *mud* (13). God likened Israel unto mud. He also called the clay, which helps make up this last evil empire, miry (or mud)! So a connection between Israel and this last evil empire can also be seen through God's selective terms **dust** and **miry**, both meaning **mud**!

The same scenario can be seen with the words *clay* and *sand*. In Daniel chapter 2, the Hebrew meaning of **clay** is *round thing (14)*. *Once again with the Abrahamic Covenant, God makes another comparison and likens His people to the sand (see Genesis 22:17, 18). Verse 17 states, "That in blessing I will bless thee, and in multiplying I will multiply thy *seed* . . . as the *sand* which is upon the sea shore." *Sand* in Genesis 22 means *as round (15)*! Both the **clay** in this evil empire and the **sand** in the descendants of Abraham have a meaning inferring **roundness**. So it is with all four descriptive words: *part, miry, potters'*, and *clay*; Israel, as well as this evil kingdom, is and will be identified.

Finally to make a comprehensive study, we must look at the second substance involved in making the image's ten toes (or ten kings of Revelation 17:12). The *STRENGTH of iron*, or the *power* of the Old Roman Empire, will mix with the miry clay. The ten toes are made of only *part* **of iron**. The Old Roman Empire split into the eastern and western divisions by Diocletian 300 A.D. Many believe the ten kings, which will unite with the Antichrist, will come from the Western Hemisphere. Notwithstanding, the multitude that followed Judas led Jesus to the Romans in the Eastern Hemisphere. The Romans in the east were given the *power* (John 19:10, 11) to flog and crucify Jesus Christ, the "temple" of God. Da. 11:31 reminds us, "And arms [Roman power] shall stand on his part, and they shall pollute the sanctuary of strength, and shall take away the daily sacrifice." The *men of the east* shall stand on Netanyahu's part, and they shall pollute the temple of God (II Thes. 2:4). It is a replica of Judas' day.

Luke 23:12 states, "And the same day Pilate [Roman Governor in the east who was *given the power*] and Herod [Jewish ruler of Galilee] **were made friends together**: for before they were at enmity between themselves." Pilate, the Roman, and Herod, the Jew, came together in **PEACE**. What are the Jews doing today? Netanyahu is signing *peace* treaties with the Arabs who live in the east. Revelation 17:12-14 tells us an evil alliance will occur among the ten kings and the Antichrist. The Arabs and the Jews, who do not mix, even as iron does not mix with clay, shall come together for a common purpose. Once again, these same evil forces will unite to come against the Lord, but this time to no avail.

"Let another take his office." Recall the quote from the *Revell Bible Dictionary*: "Judas, called the 'son of perdition' in Jn. 17:12 (KJV), is described as 'the one doomed to [eternal] destruction,' a term otherwise reserved for the Antichrist and his followers" (16). *Benjamin Netanyahu, the Antichrist, will pick up where Judas left off, at the temple.* The following information will prove this; so read it carefully. Matthew ch. 27 tells us when Judas realized he *was condemned*, (or like the Antichrist, there was no hope for him because he made a covenant with the devil), he repented himself then went to the chief priests and elders. Matthew 27:4, 5 states, "(v. 4) I have sinned in that I have betrayed the innocent blood . . . . (v. 5) And he cast down the pieces of silver in the temple, and departed." This was so symbolic to me; I could not get it off my mind. I asked the Lord, "God, why did Judas throw the money down into the temple?" When He answered, this was His response: **"Because that's where the Antichrist picks it up at."** I was astounded! Later on, God then revealed it to me in His Word.

58

THE ANTICHRIST PICKS UP THE STORY AT A "TEMPLE," LOCATED IN THE SCRIPTURES! The remainder of this chapter is dedicated to proving this point, so read it carefully. Matthew 27:9, 10 states, "(v. 9) Then was fulfilled that which was spoken by *Jeremy* the prophet, saying, And they took the *thirty pieces of silver*, the price of him that was *valued*, whom they of the children of Israel did value; (v. 10) And gave them for the *potter's field, as the Lord appointed me.*" According to the *New American Bible*, "Matthew's attributing this text to Jeremiah is puzzling, for there is no such text in that book" (17). Jeremiah never bought a field for thirty pieces of silver. Therefore, it is believed by many that Matthew is " . . . combining the Zechariah text [11:12-13, which speaks of 30 pieces of silver] with texts from Jeremiah that speak of a potter (Jer 18, 2-3), the buying of a field (Jer 32, 6-9), or the breaking of a potter's flask at Topheth in the valley of Ben-Hinnom with the prediction that it will become a *burial place* (Jer 19,1-13)" (18).

Looking at these four texts will help us to understand Matthew 27:9-10. Jeremiah 19:1-13 will be mentioned last to enhance the study. Concerning Jeremiah 18, the only point I would like to make is that God will bring evil on an unrepentant nation. The main focus of this study will be the two texts, Jeremiah 32 and Zechariah 11. These two fit perfectly together when we look at them in the light of endtime prophecy.

In Jeremiah chapter 32, the Lord, because of Judah's sin, hand delivered the land and its inhabitants over to the enemy, King Nebuchadnezzar, with the intent God would someday return it. Even so, the Lord tells Jeremiah to "buy a field," which was now in enemy territory, from his **uncle's** son Hanamel. God told Jeremiah to do this because as the *nearest relative*, he had the **right to possess the field**. Jeremiah, at the Lord's command, then *legalized* everything with written and sealed documents, calling the witnesses and weighing the money. The Word also reminds us with signs, wonders and a strong arm, God brought His people out of Egypt. He swore the Promised Land to the forefathers. The Jews today as the *"closest relatives"* have the *right of inheritance*; this land is their birthright. To understand Matthew 27:9, 10, keep in mind Jeremy's "right" to buy this field along with how he then legalized the transaction, and combine this with Zechariah 11, which speaks of *"thirty pieces of silver"* being cast into the Lord's house/temple.

Zechariah chapter 11 tells us the prophet became the good shepherd. In Zech. 11:12 the prophet stated, "If ye think good, give me my price . . . . So they weighed for my price thirty pieces of silver." Like Christ, in Matthew chapter 27:6, 9, the good shepherd was only *valued* at thirty pieces of silver, which was the price of a lamb used for the slaughter. So it was, He was not worth much to them. They did not *"value"* the good shepherd. Once the good shepherd was paid for His services, Zechariah 11:13 states, "And the LORD said unto me, Cast it unto the potter: a goodly price that I was prised at of them. And I took the thirty pieces of silver, and cast them to the potter in the house of the LORD." Here, the Lord tells the shepherd to take the thirty pieces of silver and cast it into the **temple treasury**. Thus, the money was thrown to the **"potter"** in the house of the Lord. One translation actually reads, "Throw it in the treasury" (19).

By obeying God's command, the prophet portrayed Jesus Christ as well as Judas Iscariot:

A) Christ was *"valued"* at thirty pieces of silver, the price of a *lamb* used for slaughter. In Ex. 21:32, when a *man's servant* was killed by another's ox, the man who owned the ox had to pay the other thirty shekels of silver for the death of the servant. Jesus Christ ". . . took upon him the form of a *servant"* (Phil. 2:7). Judas received *sacrificial money* for the death of a servant. Christ was the *Lamb* to be slain from the foundations of the world (Rev. 13:8).

B) The prophet also foreshadowed the action of Judas Iscariot, in Matthew chapter 27:5, when Judas had cast the thirty pieces of silver down into the temple. However in Zech. 11, the story is slightly different from the one concerning Judas in Matt. 27.

The reader can now combine the texts Jer. 32 and Zech. 11,

derived from Matt. 27:9,10, to give us a full understanding of endtime events. Recall in Matt. 27:6 it was *"UNLAWFUL"* for the chief priest to accept Judas' wages and put it into the **treasury** because it was the "**price of blood**." Yet in Zechariah 11:13, the money is put into the temple treasury. *The prophet put the blood money into the temple treasury to signify that an "unlawful act" just took place.* Understand, in Jeremiah 32, Jeremy had the right, as the nearest relative to possess the land. The "field" was Jeremy's birthright, and the transaction was *"**LEGALLY SEALED**."* When Benjamin Netanyahu "sold out" the Jews' inherited land, he committed an "*__UNLAWFUL ACT__*," for the Jews have the right as the nearest relative to possess the land.

Nevertheless, Netanyahu did not *value* his people, like the Jews did not value Christ in Matt. 27:9 and this is why the prophet threw the thirty pieces of silver into the temple treasury. This action signified the Jewish people, like Christ, becoming as sheep for the slaughter. In dealing with their inheritance and not "valuing" the flock, Benjamin Netanyahu will bring the bloodshed to God's sheep. When he gave away the Jews' inherited land of Hebron, Netanyahu set up the Israelis as sheep for the slaughter. They are now totally surrounded by their enemy and without sufficient protection.

In not valuing the flock, the Israeli Prime Minister, a foolish shepherd, has picked up the thirty pieces of silver and *purchased a "field of blood*." You might be thinking, but Matthew 27:5-8 states, "(v. 5) And he [Judas] cast down the pieces of silver in the temple . . . . (v. 6) And the *chief priests took the silver pieces . . .* (v. 7) *and bought with them the potter's field . . .* (v. 8) *called, The field of blood . . . .* " In contrast, Luke in Acts 1:18, depicts Judas as the one who, *WITH HIS BETRAYAL MONEY*, buys the field of blood. One translation of Acts 1:18, 19 reads, "He [Judas] bought a parcel of land with the "WAGES OF HIS INIQUITY" . . . the parcel of land was [also] called . . . Field of Blood" (20). Matthew chapter 27, along with Acts chapter 1, agrees only in the purchase of the field of blood and that the field was bought with the *betrayal money*. *__THE BETRAYAL MONEY IS THE KEY__*! Matthew tells us Judas threw the **MONEY** down at the temple, so how in the world did Judas pick up the **WAGES** to go and buy the field?! He did not, but the Antichrist did! The *money* was in Benjamin Netanyahu's hand. Acts chapter 1 was purposely written to portray the Antichrist's actions of buying the field. It is Benjamin Netanyahu who has bought the field of blood "*with the WAGES of iniquity*!" He has picked up the "pieces" where Judas threw them down, at the temple!

> *Lord, why did Judas throw the thirty pieces of silver down into the temple?*
>
> *Because that's where the Antichrist picks them up!!!*

For confirmation of Netanyahu's unlawful dealings, look at the transition that takes place after the prophet tossed the thirty pieces of silver into the treasury. Zechariah 11:14-17 states:

> (v. 14) Then I cut asunder mine other staff, even Bands, [**Bands in the Hebrew means _deal, inheritance (21)_**] that I might **break the brotherhood between Judah and Israel.** [*Right now Judah is applying for a separate state, due to Benjamin Netanyahu making a deal with their inherited land, Hebron.*] (v. 15) And the LORD said unto me, Take unto thee yet the instruments [armour (22)] of a foolish shepherd [Netanyahu, Israel's leader]. (v. 16) For, lo, I will raise up a shepherd in the land, which shall not visit those that be cut off, neither shall seek the young one, nor heal that that is broken, nor feed that that standeth still [**he does not "_value_" the flock**]: but he shall eat the flesh of the fat, and tear their claws in pieces. (v. 17) Woe to the idol shepherd that **leaveth the flock** [they are as sheep for the slaughter]! the sword shall be upon his arm, and upon his right eye: his arm shall be clean dried up, and his right eye shall be utterly darkened.

Then in the very next chapter, and man placed chapters in the scripture, Jerusalem becomes ". . . a cup of trembling . . . a burdensome stone for all people . . ." (Zechariah 12:2, 3).

God is telling us in these last days He will raise up a false shepherd, who like Judas, will not "value" the flock. This man will do the unlawful by dealing with the Jews' inherited land. The Prime Minister's action has caused strife amongst the

Jewish people. Like Christ, they will become as sheep for the slaughter. David Wilder, a spokesman for the settlers in Hebron stated, "**This agreement is suicide**. It is dangerous not only for the Jewish community of Hebron, it is dangerous for Israel as a whole" (23). Jimmy Deyoung Jr., a journalist stationed in Jerusalem, Israel, stated:

> . . . the 140,000 settlers in Judah were dedicated campaigners for Netanyahu; that's what got him elected. Now they're going to turn against him. And I want to tell you something: *I hold right here in my hand the constitution to a second state of Jewish people in the land of Israel.* This is the constitution for the state of Judah. Check out sometime the book of Ezekiel 37:15-24, where it says there will be two Jewish states in the land at the time of the end, Israel and Judah. CNN had a commentator the day of the elections last May who said now the Jews are dividing back into their twelve tribes. They have the constitution. *They are set ready to go with this decision by Netanyahu on Hebron.* He has divided those people even more so. (24)

Recall from the beginning of this study, Jeremiah 19:1-13, which speaks of a burial place and was also associated with Matthew 27:9-10. Jeremiah 19 reiterates the story. Here we find the Lord is going to *bring evil* upon the Israelites because they have *forsaken Him*. They had *estranged the land* and had filled it with the *blood of innocence*. Jeremiah 19:5, 6 states, "[v. 5] They have built high places for Baal to immolate their sons in fire as *holocausts* to Baal: [they did not value the flock] . . . . [v. 6] Therefore, days will come, says the LORD, when this place will no longer be called Topheth, [also known by some as the potter's field (25)] . . . but rather, the **Valley of *Slaughter*** [the Jews will be as sheep for the slaughter] . . . . [v. 11] And Topheth shall be a burial place . . ." (26).

This chart will help you recall the material that has been discussed:

Son of Perdition

Judas	Antichrist
1) Sold out Jesus (temple) and Apostles.	1) Netanyahu sells out temple/country.
2) Had prominent position, i.e., treasurer.	2) Netanyahu is prime minister.
3) Supplied their needs as treasurer.	3) Netanyahu is an economist and wants to turn economy around.
4) Jews trusted him because of his position.	4) Jews will trust in their prime minister.
5) The apostles never saw the betrayal coming.	5) Jews will not see betrayal coming.
6) Sold out his birthright. Set the Lamb up to be slain.	6) Surrendered his birthright and set the sheep up for slaughter.
7) Betrayed Jesus. Spoke lies at a table. It did not prosper.	7) Betrays country. Speaks lies at a table. But it shall not prosper (Dan. 11:27).
8) Judas betrayed the cause.	8) The Antichrist will sell out the cause betraying his country (Dan. 11).
9) He was "guide" for Jews, and Romans in desecrating Jesus/temple and bringing Him to destruction.	9) He will be "guide" for Jews and ten kings (Arabs), which desecrate the temple.
10) Son of Perdition, meaning "the one doomed to [eternal] destruction" (John 17:12).	10) Son of Perdition (II Thess. 2:3).
11) One hour of power (Luke 22:53).	11) One hour of power (Rev. 17:12).
12) The beast "that was" (Rev. 17:8).	12) "Is not" and "yet is."
13) Did not value Jesus or the apostles.	13) Netanyahu (Idol Shepherd) does not value the flock.
14) He was grieved (Matt. 27:3-5).	14) Netanyahu will be grieved (Dan. 11).

15) Cast 30 pieces of silver into temple (Matt. 27:5).	15) Netanyahu picks up 30 pieces of silver and does the unlawful.
16) Smite the shepherd, sheep will scatter (Zechariah 13:7).	16) Stands in holy place (temple), flock warned in Judea to flee (Matt. 24:15-21).
17) Feet with ten toes (part iron and part clay) (Dan. 2:41-43). Judas helped bring together Romans and Jews.	17) Ten kings (Romans/Arabs coming together with Jews) (Rev. 17:12).
18) Genesis 22:17 and 28:14, referred to the Abrahamic Covenant. Here God likens the Jews, to whom He gave the Promised Land, as to the *sand - as round *dust – mud	18) Dan. 2:41-43 – evil empire. Feet and toes of iron and clay Part iron – former E. Roman Empire Part clay - Israelis are still God's people Potter – the LORD *clay – round thing *miry – mud
19) Pilate and Herod were at "enmity," but they made peace, (Luke 23:12).	19) Arafat/Arabs and Netanyahu/Jews are coming together in "peace."

Chapter 5
These Two Are One

Rebekah, Isaac's wife, was to deliver twin boys, Esau and Jacob, (see Genesis 25:19-34) The LORD referred to these boys as *two nations that struggled* within the womb. The younger boy, **Jacob**, later named **Israel**, would be the stronger of the two and the elder son, Esau, would serve the younger. An article titled "The Jews Come Home [-] Return From Exile" states, ". . . there is a good deal of evidence that the **Palestinian people** who live in the land today could be descendants of **Esau**" (1). According to later Assyrian and Babylonian records, part of Palestine was known as the land of the Hatti, which is Hittites. By Abraham's time, many Hittite people had settled in Canaan. When Esau was forty, he married two Hittite women, which grieved Isaac and Rebekah. Esau had been warned not to take a wife from the land of Canaan, due to their idolatry and lack of morality. Nevertheless, again in Genesis 28:8, 9 we find, "(v. 8) And Esau seeing that the daughters of Canaan pleased not Isaac his father; (v. 9) Then went Esau unto Ishmael, and took unto the wives which he had Mahalath the daughter of Ishmael Abraham's son." Scholar Victor Mordecai says, "Esau lived thereafter with his Uncle Ishmael" (2).

Ishmael, being the father of the Arab nations, lived in a land full of oil. And Isaac, when he bestowed his blessing upon Esau prophesied, "Behold, **of the fat places of the earth shall be thy dwelling** (fat places in Hebrew literally means '**of the oils of the land!**'). And of the dew of heaven from above (meaning the **desert**)" (3). When looking at Esau's dwelling place along with whom he married, it becomes apparent Esau together with Ishmael are the forefathers of the Arab and Muslim peoples.

These two nations, to whom Rebekah gave birth, are still struggling today. With adversity on every side, the Jews yet remain grounded by the hand of God. God told Abram, concerning the land of Canaan, that He would bless him and make a great nation of him. In Genesis 27:29, Jacob/Israel was blessed by Isaac and was told, "Let people serve thee, and nations bow down to thee: **be lord over thy brethren**, and let thy mother's sons bow down to thee." God has blessed the Jewish people by giving them the Promised Land, increasing their financial means, and strengthening their military ability. The Palestinians, on the other hand, have a strong desire for the God-given land, depend on Israel for financial gain, and still seek autonomy in the region. The following statement from a September 30, 1996, *St. Petersburg Times* article provides an example of Israel's current power of authority over Palestine:

> Israel is guilty of provoking an incitement . . . by again reneging on agreements, by bottling up the Palestinians, by placing us in a state of siege, by threatening all the time, by destroying our economy . . . . He [Netanyahu] used force to prevent the Palestinian government from doing business in East Jerusalem . . . [and], postponed a promised Israeli withdrawal from Hebron . . . . (4)

But how long can the Nation of Israel maintain the upper hand? In Genesis 27:40, *Isaac tells Esau*, "And by thy sword shalt thou live, and shalt serve thy brother; and it shall come to pass when thou shalt have the dominion, that thou *shalt break his yolk from off thy neck*." We are living in that present day. In the very near future, the Jewish people will be under the control of an Arab/Muslim coalition. Make no mistake about it,

1) THERE IS A DEFINITE CORRELATION BETWEEN ESAU AND THE TEN HORNS/BEAST OF REVELATION 17:3.

2) AND BETWEEN JACOB AND THE ANTICHRIST/BEAST IN REVELATION 17:12.

To better understand the connection between the two entities, consider their similarities. To begin with, let's look briefly at some of the words used to describe the subject matter and the names selected for them. Names were very important in the Bible. In biblical times, names were used to make statements about one's character. They were an extension or an expression of the individual. Many times a name was changed when a person's behavior or status changed. Abram was a good example of this; his name was changed to Abraham when God gave the promise.

To properly display the connection between Esau and that of the beast, or the ten Arab kings of Revelation 17, a brief study comparing the similarities of their names, and character is in order. Let us begin by studying Esau, the first part of this equation. Genesis chapter 25:25, 27 states, "(v. 25) And the **first** came out red, all over *like* an **hairy garment**; and they called his name **Esau**. (v. 27) [A]nd Esau was a cunning **hunter, a man of the field**." Genesis 25:30 says he was later named **Edom**. He was known for being "**hairy**"; see Gen. 27:11.

1) <u>First</u> - beginning (5).
2) <u>Hairy</u> - meaning hurl as a storm, be tempestuous, come like (take away as with) a whirlwind (6).
3) <u>Garment</u> - meaning something ample, powerful (7).
4) <u>Esau</u> - rough, **deal (with)** (8).
5) <u>Hunter</u> - to lie alongside (i.e. in wait) (9).
6) <u>Man</u> - "of the field."
7) <u>Edom</u> - red (10).
8) <u>Hairy</u> - devil (11).

<u>In Revelation chapter 17, the Greek definition of the word 'beast' is almost identical to the Hebrew definitions of those words previously used to describe Esau's name and character</u>. Note the resemblance, which the beast has with Esau. The word beast in the Greek means a dangerous *animal*, (wild **[rough, stormy, tempestuous, turbulent (12) (swirling (13))]** beast) (14). The definition of 'beast' is a lower animal as distinguished from man <beasts "**of the field**">, **syn. brute** (15), **hunting, trap** (16). Look at the parallels in Gen. 25:25, 26: "(v. 25) And the *first* came out red, all over like an hairy garment; and they called his name Esau. (v. 26) And after that came his brother out . . . ." In the same fashion as Esau, the ten kings will also be *first born* and *then* the Antichrist will follow. Daniel 7:24 confirms this: "And the ten horns out of this kingdom are ten kings that shall arise: and another [Netanyahu] shall rise *after* them."

Esau, the *firstborn* child, was to receive a double proportion of his father's estate. As the eldest son, he *was to receive the covenant promises God gave* to his father's father, Abraham. However, over a bowl of some red pottage, Esau sold his birthright to his younger brother Jacob. We find this in Gen. 25, where Jacob, in order to tempt Esau into giving away his birthright, **sod pottage** (meaning "**to deal**," refer to pg.73), and Esau being faint from the field wanted what Jacob had to offer. Esau's name means *deal with*. Esau's heart desired to make a deal with his brother. Hence, he said, *"Feed me, I "pray" thee, with that same red pottage"* (Gen. 25:30). Esau wanted to partake of Jacob's offering. The *desire of his heart* was all it took to get his *name changed* to Edom meaning **red**. The beast in Rev. 17:3 was also scarlet or red in color. Esau's name change showed forth a status change, one now of union and participation with the beast.

Tempted by hunger, Esau was now where Jacob wanted him. Jacob then asked Esau to sell him his birthright. Not valuing his birthright, Esau surrendered it over to Jacob. Esau stated in Genesis 25:32-34, "(v. 32) Behold, I am at the point to *die*: and what profit shall this birthright do to me? (v. 33) And Jacob said, Swear to me this day; and he *sware* unto him: and he sold his birthright unto Jacob . . . (v. 34) and he did *eat and drink* . . . thus Esau *despised* his birthright." Once Esau handed over the right to receive the covenant promises of God, he was then allowed to *eat and drink*. Afterward, Esau *despised* his birthright.

Similarly, the beast, a terribly strong hostile power controlled by the devil, will hate or *despise* the things of God. In the last days, a tempting proposal will be stirring in the pot. According to Rev. 13, the day will come when no man will be able to buy or sell unless he takes the mark of the beast. Like Esau, feeling a "little faint," the person may say in his heart, I want to be fed. I want to partake of the offer. The beast will then *ask* of him or her to take his mark, or in other words, *marry him*. When a person agrees to taking the mark of the beast, he or she will be saying, "I do" to a proposal of marriage. Thus, as a bride to her groom, he or she will eventually turn over the gift of the birthright unto the beast. In wanting the individual to be totally committed to the promise, the beast will then say, *swear* it unto me. He will lead the individual to an "*altar*" of marriage, and whosoever shall *take his mark* will "*worship*" the beast and his "*image*," (Rev. 14:9).

The beast's mark, going into the right hand or forehead, will be his acceptance of the bride; his wedding gift will enable the individual to "eat and drink." Thereafter, as with any marriage, the *dual expression of acceptance makes them one.* In making such a pledge, the individual, will then "*despise*" the things of God. (Note: *A MARRIAGE IS A COVENANT*, [see Jer. 31:32, Mal. 2:13-16].) God warns us not to marry the enemy, but destroy his *altars*, break his *images* and *not worship* any other god (**Ex. 34:10-17).

It's time to study the other half of the equation, which is Jacob and how he represents the Antichrist. But first, think about this: later on in his life, Jacob had to have his "name changed" to Israel because he could not represent God as a deceiver or supplanter. So, *when referring to Jacob as representing the Antichrist, this would be prior to his name change.* Daniel 7:24 states, "And the ten horns out of this kingdom are ten kings [Arabs/Esau] that shall arise: and another [Netanyahu] shall rise **after** them; **and he shall be *diverse* from the first**." Netanyahu is *diverse.* He is a Jew as opposed to an Arab.

Genesis 25:26 states the following concerning the twin boys' birth: "And after that [Esau's birth] came his brother out, and his hand took hold on Esau's heel; and his name was called Jacob." Jacob's hand taking hold of Esau's heel denoted **he will have the dominion in this relationship, and *together* they will bring about a sequence of events**. Revelation 17:13 states the same thing concerning the Antichrist and the ten kings. The Antichrist, like Jacob, will have the **dominant role in the relationship**; Benjamin Netanyahu along with the ten kings shall *have one mind* bringing about a sequence of events. (Note: The story of the tabernacle, as will be discussed later, shows the Arabs and the Jews being "*coupled together*" by means of evil spells. Interestingly enough, in Genesis 25:24, these boys were referred to as twins, and twins in the Hebrew means *coupled together*) (17).

71

To further strengthen the statement previous, just study Jacob's name which is an extension or an expression of his character. **JACOB MEANS SUPPLANTER** (18). This is extremely important because the term supplant was derived from subunder and planta, or *SOLE* OF THE FOOT! (19). UNDERSTAND, JACOB IS THE BASE OR FOUNDATION UPON WHICH THE TEN ARAB KINGS WILL STAND. In Daniel 2, Nebuchadnezzar, the king of Babylon, had a troublesome dream of an image which Daniel gave the interpretation thereof. This dramatic prophetic occurrence shows the path of history from that time forward and hereafter. Five world empires are in the dream, four of which have already fallen; the other is still to come. The fifth and final kingdom before Christ returns, is known as the *"FEET (FOOT)"* of the image. We are living in the days of the feet. The <u>ten toes</u> on the image's feet represent the <u>ten Arab kings</u>. **JACOB, THE ANTICHRIST OR *SUPPLANTER*, IS THE *"SOLE"* UPON WHICH THE TEN KINGS SHALL STAND!**

In Gen. 27:35 Isaac tells Esau, "And he said, Thy brother came with subtilty, and hath taken away thy blessing." *Strong's Exhaustive Concordance* defines subtilty as: deceiving, fraud, treachery, to delude, betray, etc. (20). Jacob and Benjamin Netanyahu have the same nature. This will be expressed throughout the remainder of the story.

The Bible, in Genesis 25:27, says Jacob was a *plain (pious (21)) man*, meaning he pretended religious devotion. Definitely, the Prime Minister has shown a "religious swing" in his step. This becomes apparent when observing his actions. After getting the final results to the elections, Netanyahu went straight to the Western Wall to pray. Once elected, "He had forged a six-party ruling coalition whose conservative tilt could . . . *refashion religious* and social affairs in the Jewish state" (22).

Before his election, Benjamin Netanyahu and his Party had demonized Yasser Arafat. Bibi proclaimed he would NOT meet with Arafat and there would be NO withdrawal of troops from Hebron. But remember what the Prophet Daniel said, "And after the league made with him he shall work deceitfully" (Da. 11:23). Ironically, not even five months into office, Netanyahu shook

72

hands with Yasser Arafat, a bloodthirsty man who has only one goal, to obtain the *city of Jerusalem*. "Pious" Bibi states, "We think that peace and prosperity go hand in hand -- I believe we can advance and achieve both goals for the benefit of both peoples" (23).

According to columnist George F. Will's editorial, "Netanyahu Sticks to His Promise," "Netanyahu's guidelines say Israeli settlements in the West Bank and elsewhere are important for defense and '*Zionist fulfillment*'" (24). Portraying himself to be a "religious person" will enhance Netanyahu's acceptance as Messiah. Rabbi Chaim Richman, the Director for Public Affairs at the Temple Institute stated, "The Messiah is a person who has a certain task to fulfill . . . the kingdom to be restored to Israel, the temple to be rebuilt, *the ingathering of the exiles*, the complete obliteration of evil from the world . . . a descendant of David but also completely human, a regular human being who is the greatest political leader who ever lived" (25). *Prophecy is being fulfilled before our very eyes, as Bibi creates and fulfills Israel's Zionist dream.* He is right now preparing for the *exiles* to come home. New settlements are going up in many areas, such as the Old City, parts of East Jerusalem and parts of the West Bank; "[he has also] renew[ed] a dormant financial subsidy program to lure thousands more settlers to the region" (26). However, it is all just an act of deception.

> *Special Note: Before studying the following verses, one must understand **Esau sold his *birthright*** to Jacob, Israel, long ago. Therefore, in order to look accurately and prophetically at this story, we must see the birthright today as lying in the hands of Jacob. ***Now Israel is the one selling out her birthright***.

Genesis chapter 25:29 and 30 states, "And Jacob [the Antichrist] **SOD POTTAGE**: and Esau [the Arabs] came from the field, and he was faint: And Esau said to Jacob, Feed me, I pray thee, with that **SAME RED POTTAGE**; for I am faint: therefore was his name called Edom."

> 1) **sod** means to seethe; i.e., (**to boil** (27)), **deal** proudly, insolent (**dictatorial** (28)) (29).
> 2) **pottage** means to seethe or (**to boil**), **deal** proudly (30).

3) **red** describing the pottage means to **show blood** (31).
Lying beneath the **BOILING** broth, there is a **DEAL**, which will
turn to **BLOOD**. Peering deeply into the **POT** will allow one to
view the **CHOPPED PIECES** of **SKIN** and **BONES** brewing in
blood. These are the bodies of the Jewish people as well as the
leaders who *deal with* the division of Israel's birthright, the land.
**Ironically Benjamin Netanyahu, showing he is dictatorial,
stated, "'I would be very careful before I would *add* more *cooks*
to the *broth* [death in the pot] -- I can't think that at this time in
such sensitive *negotiations* it would be wise to introduce another
interlocutor'" (32). These leaders, who partake of this *same red
pottage*, *will become what they eat*, for eating is a powerful
symbol in the Bible that portrays **participation** and **unification**,
(i.e., II Kings 4:38-40). Eating of the same red pottage, these
leaders will form into the scarlet colored beast of Revelation
chapter 17.

As with Jacob and Esau, the **_birthright_** remains the basis of
the **negotiations**. The *land* for peace *deal* is boiling in the *pot*,
and the smoke is billowing in God's face. The *Revell Bible
Dictionary* says, "Micah carefully details the sins that make
divine judgment certain (2:1, 2; 3:1-7; 6:9 - 7:6)" (33). In Micah
chapter 3, God warns the *rulers of Israel* who love sin. Verses 3
and 5 state,

> (v. 3) Who also **EAT** the **FLESH** of my people, and
> **FLAY THEIR SKIN** from off them; and they **BREAK
> THEIR BONES**, and **CHOP THEM IN PIECES**, <u>AS
> FOR THE "POT"</u> . . . . (v. 5) Thus saith the LORD
> concerning the prophets that make my people err, that bite
> with their teeth, and cry, **PEACE** [*their negotiating the
> birthright*]; and he that putteth not into their mouths, they
> even prepare war against him.

Israeli and Arab leaders cry peace in negotiating the birthright,
and in the last days, they will make war against the Lamb.
Micah 3:8, 10 states, "(v. 8) But truly I am full of power by the
spirit of the LORD, and of judgment, and of might, to declare
unto *Jacob* his transgression, and to Israel his sin . . . . (v. 10)
"THEY" BUILD UP ZION WITH BLOOD."
Micah 2:1-4 states the following:

(v. 1) Woe to them that devise iniquity, and work evil upon their beds! when the morning is light, they [leaders] practise it, because it is in the power of their hand. (v. 2) And they *covet fields, and take them by violence*; and houses, and take them away: so they oppress a man and his house, even a man and his *heritage*. (v. 3) Therefore thus saith the LORD; Behold, against this family do I devise an evil, from which ye shall not remove your necks; neither shall ye go haughtily: for this time is evil. (v. 4) In that day shall one take up a parable against you, and lament with a doleful lamentation, and say, We be utterly spoiled: **he** [Netanyahu] hath changed the portion of my people: how hath he removed it from me! *turning away* he hath *divided* our *fields*.

Doesn't this sound like betrayal?

Micah chapter 7 talks of an evil time when rulers take bribes and a man's enemy is of his own house, betrayal. Verse 4 states, " . . . the day of thy watchmen and thy visitation cometh . . . . " As the first Prime Minister of Israel to be elected, via the public, it is said that Bibi has more power in his hands than any of the previous rulers. In Daniel 11:30, we see the Antichrist "returns" (or lodges), for a period of time, only to make a final decision of betrayal to his country. He then, with an army, comes back and **_with violence takes Israel's heritage from her_**: "Woe to them that devise iniquity, and work evil **upon their beds!** when the morning is light, they practise it, because it is in the power of their hand. And they covet fields, and take them by violence; and houses, and take them away: so they oppress a man and his house, even a man and his heritage" (Micah 2:1-2).

The perpetual event of Israeli leaders giving away their heritage started with the former Prime Minister Yitzhak Rabin and will soon end with Benjamin Netanyahu, but not until their appointed time. For now, the Prime Minister stirs the pot. He uses wit and cunning craftiness to *tempt* Arafat. In an attempt to get what he wants, Bibi has tempted Yasser Arafat with meaningless dialogue, mingled with stalling tactics. In the meantime, he created Jewish settlements in the West Bank and elsewhere. He also conducted a surprise excavation tunnel below the edge of the temple mount. This was extremely disturbing to the Muslims. The site is sacred to them because it holds the Dome of the Rock and al-Aqsa mosque. To the Jews, it is where Solomon built the temple. The *St. Petersburg Times* reported that "Muslim clerics said the tunnel runs underneath the Temple Mount complex and has endangered the stability of the buildings above. They also said they feared the tunnel was a *first step* by Israel toward tearing down the two Muslim sites and rebuilding the temple" (34). The excavation triggered an outbreak of fighting that left 70 people dead in the region. Netanyahu accused the Palestinian leaders of inciting the riots with "wild and unfounded accusations." "This is a very dangerous game, and I do not advise anyone to play it" (35); Netanyahu, being quite bold with his statements, is determined to get what he wants. Shortly after the uprising, Benjamin Netanyahu, Yasser Arafat and King Hussein of Jordan, met at the White House for a two day summit. Nothing worthwhile was resolved, and Arafat went home with what he came with, a promise to talk again.

Then on January 15, 1997, Benjamin Netanyahu and his cabinet agreed with the previous peace treaty in surrendering over Hebron, the Jews inherited land, to the Palestinians. The brew is now boiling in the pot, and the blood is soon to show. God will allow evil to come upon unbelieving Israel. **A time known as "Jacob's trouble" will prepare them for Christ's coming and the receiving of their promised kingdom on earth**. To thoroughly understand the following verses we must first realize that *"Jacob" has a double meaning*. To prove this, think about the word *"him"* in the following verses from Jeremiah 30:7-9:

> (v. 7) Alas! for that day is great, so that none is like it: it is even the time of Jacob's [Antichrist's] trouble [tribulation (36)]; but he [Israel] shall be saved out of it. [Recall Jacob is symbolic for the Antichrist before his name changed to Israel.] (v. 8) For it shall come to pass in that day, saith the LORD of hosts, that I will break his

yoke from off thy neck, and will burst thy bonds, and strangers shall no more serve themselves of <u>HIM</u> [Jacob/Benjamin]: (v. 9) But they shall serve the LORD their God.

The word "him," refers to whom in this verse? Since there is no other name mentioned, it has to be Jacob!

Chapter 6
And Jacob Stated, "I AM!"

Being old in age, his eyes dim to where he could not see, Isaac prepared for his "**unknown**" day of death. He wanted to pass his blessing from God down to his eldest son Esau. However, before Isaac would pass his blessing on, he just had to eat of the venison that "he so loved." Therefore, he sent Esau out to hunt for it. This venison, also called savory meat, was something quite special to Isaac, for he *greatly desired* and loved to eat it. The Bible really emphasized his love for this venison on three different occasions (see Genesis 27:4, 9 and 14). Surely it was *customary* for Isaac to eat this meat, for everyone knew how he loved and cherished it. He just had to have it *before* he would pass on the blessing.

This particular biography offers a wonderful insight into God's plan of the ages. Isaac, being a forefather of the Jewish nation, represents certain Jews in Israel, and the *__venison__*, he "so loved," represents the *__temple__* these Jews desire. Venison means provision (1) and provision means *something provided for the future* (2). Many Jews believe whoever *provides* the temple and brings peace will be their Messiah. When Bibi brings the provision, the Israelis' temple, Israel, like Isaac, will be unable to discern the identity of their leader. In preparing for their "unknown" day of death, the Israelis will partake of the deception and then *bless* Netanyahu with the spiritual blessing. Gershon Salomon, head of the Temple Mount Faithful states, " ' . . . Israel is weak. They are ready to *give everything*, even for a false peace . . . . *The main thing they pray about is asking God to rebuild the Third Temple* . . . for most of the Israelis, *__it is a desire, a deep desire__* ' " (3).

Gen. 27:5-13 tells us Isaac's wife Rebekah and Jacob, his younger son, conspired together to deceive Isaac so Jacob could receive Esau's blessing. Rebekah commanded her son to quickly go and kill two kid goats. She would then prepare them as if they were the venison. Gen. 27:14-16 tells the story:

(v. 14) And he went, and fetched, and brought them to his

mother: and his mother made savoury meat, such as his father loved. (v. 15) And Rebekah took **goodly** [*to COVET, desire* (4)] **raiment** [*TREACHERY or pillage* (5) *(pillage means plunder* (6) *[to rob;* **TO TAKE (PROPERTY) BY FORCE OR FRAUD** (7)])] of her eldest son Esau . . . and put them upon Jacob her younger son: (v. 16) And she put the skins [*to be made naked* (8)] of the kids of the goats upon his hands, and upon the smooth of his neck.

Notice the deceit that is taking place here. *Jacob "put on" Esau's goodly raiment*, and that's the key. Because of his heart's *desire*, Benjamin Netanyahu will "put on" Arab garments. He will wear the garments of **COVETOUSNESS**. He, along with the Arabs, will **TAKE ISRAEL'S PROPERTY BY FORCE OR BY FRAUD**, thereby committing **TREASON** before his country (see also Micah 2 on pgs. 74-75). Once this happens, Benjamin will **be made naked** before the Lord. Like Jacob, Netanyahu will put on goat's hair to deceive and receive his spiritual blessing. He will become what the Arabs are, to get what he wants!

The story continues in Gen. 27:18-20:

(v. 18) And he came unto his father, and said, My father: and he said, Here am I; who art thou, my son? (v. 19) And Jacob said unto his father, I am Esau thy firstborn; I have done according as thou badest me: arise, I pray thee, sit and eat of my venison [or what I have "provided" for you], that thy soul may bless me. (v. 20) And Isaac said unto his son, How is it that thou hast found it so quickly, my son? And he said, Because the **LORD THY GOD** *BROUGHT* it to me.

Jacob was telling his father that *God brought* the venison to him to give to his father. The word "*brought*," in this particular verse, is extremely important. Throughout the whole entire Bible, this is the only time the word *brought* means the following: **TO BRING ABOUT, SPECIFICALLY TO IMPOSE TIMBERS (FOR ROOF OR FLOOR): LAY (MAKE) BEAMS** (9). This is a temple! Venison means something provided for the future. This verse is telling us the temple the Jews so desire will be provided for them. As with Jacob, Benjamin Netanyahu will establish a "temple" or in essence a *house of authority* in the Jewish community, and they will wonder at the site. When asked how it was that he did this thing, Benjamin Netanyahu will reply, "**THE LORD THY *GOD BROUGHT* IT**." Prophetically speaking, Netanyahu will claim that he is God because he will bring the temple unto Israel.

Genesis 27:21-24 also tells us how Jacob tricked his father:

> (v. 21) And Isaac said unto Jacob, Come near, I pray thee, that I may *feel thee*, my son, whether thou be my very son [anointed one (10)] Esau or not. (v. 22) And **JACOB** went near unto Isaac his father; and he felt him . . . . (v. 23) *And he discerned him not* . . . *so he blessed him*. (v. 24) And he said, Art thou my very son Esau? [Who is firstborn, to be the leader and priest?]   And he [Jacob/Benjamin] said, **I AM**.

The Antichrist, like Jacob before he had received his name change, will be a liar and a deceiver. The Jewish people, being blind to their prime minister's performance, will act upon what they *feel*. When they ask Benjamin Netanyahu, "Are you our anointed one, the King, who will restore the kingdom to Israel?" He, like Jacob, will reply, "**I AM**." Then, as Judas did with Jesus, Jacob kissed his father with the kiss of death.

Chapter 7
Firstborn

As was stated before hand, the Antichrist, or the ruler of the Hebrew Nation, will sit in the temple of God and claim to be God. He will claim to be the High Priest. He will say, "I am the promised King *and* Priest because I follow after the 'order of Melchizedek.'" Melchizedek was the king and priest of Salem, or modern day Jerusalem, back in the days of Abraham (Gen. 14:18, Heb. 7:1, 2). Melchizedek, the Bible says, had no beginning, no ending and was without parents. Only God has no beginning and no ending. God came to the earth in the form of a king and a priest. We find more information about this in the *Holman Bible Dictionary for Windows*:

> Psalms 110:4 refers to **one** who would be *forever* a priest in the "order of Melchizedek." <u>This messianic psalm teaches that the leader or ruler of the *Hebrew nation* would be able to reflect *in his person* the role of *priest* as well as the role of *king*</u>. The writer of Hebrews made several references in chapters 5-7 to Jesus' priesthood being of the "order of Melchizedek" as opposed to Levitical in nature. The author of Hebrews cited Psalm 110:4. For the writer of Hebrews, only Jesus whose life could not be destroyed by death fit the psalmist's description of a priest of the "order of Melchizedek." (1)

The Jews, however, did not accept Jesus as King and Priest. Therefore, they are looking for another. They will look to Benjamin Netanyahu to fulfill the "needed" role of King and Priest. An understanding of the "firstborn" child's role in Israel will clarify this.

In Israel, the firstborn child of every family played an extremely important role in the Old Testament. ***The firstborn was holy unto God. They were set apart to serve as priests for the family or the clan***. That's why Jacob, in Genesis 25:31, 33, was *bargaining with the firstborn son Esau to get his birthright*. Jacob said unto his brother "(v. 31) . . . Sell me this day thy birthright. (v. 32) And Esau said, Behold, I am at the point to die: and what profit shall this birthright do to me? . . . (v. 33) and he sold his birthright unto Jacob." Jacob understood when he received Esau's birthright with it came special inheritance rights. Upon the death of the firstborn's father, the recipient would receive a **_double portion of the family's estate_**, and the **_family's lineage_** was to be passed down through him.

It is through the lineage of Isaac, Esau and Jacob's father, that the _priestly heritage_ becomes evident. Isaac's father Abraham was given several covenant promises from God. One promise was the seed of righteousness, or Jesus Christ the "**High Priest**" would come through the seed of Isaac (Gen. 21:12). Interestingly enough however, Abraham's son Isaac was not the firstborn child. Abraham's other son Ishmael was the firstborn. According to the law, Ishmael was actually in line to receive the birthright, and thus, the priesthood should have come through his loins. Yet, Isaac was entitled to the **priestly heritage** because he was a _"firstborn"_ of the promise. The seed of righteousness, or the priesthood, was going to come through Isaac's family lineage. *__The term firstborn has a *double meaning,* and this will be discussed throughout the remainder of this chapter__.

Ishmael was a _"firstborn"_ of the flesh. Isaac was the _"firstborn"_ of the Spirit. Isaac was known as the son of promise (see Romans 9:7, 8). Christ was known as the promised son. Therefore, Isaac would then follow after the _"order"_ of Jesus Christ as _the "firstborn" of the resurrection_. Like Christ, Isaac was called the "only begotten," the **_ONLY_ born _SON_ of his father**. When you are an only son, you are a firstborn. Zechariah 12:10 uses these terms in conjunction: " . . . and they shall mourn for him [Jesus Christ], as one mourneth for his **only son**, and shall be in bitterness for him, as one that is in bitterness for his **firstborn**."

Following the order of Christ, the children of Israel, _who came from the seed of Isaac_, were also known as the _"firstborn."_ They were to serve as a _kingdom of priests_, and a holy nation (see Exodus 4:22; 19:6). (Understand, however, Israel was _cut off_ from having that position, and now they must go to the Father to be resurrected from the dead [note last chapter].) The birthright today goes to whoever will receive Christ. The church, like Christ and Isaac, is the firstborn. We are " . . . a **royal priesthood**, a holy nation . . ." (Rom. 8:28-29, I Peter 2:9). Galatians 3:29 states, "And if ye be Christ's, then are ye Abraham's *seed*, and heirs according to the promise." We who are in Christ have become the sons of God and heirs to the Lord's estate (John 1 & James 2:5).

Benjamin Netanyahu is the *first* Prime Minister *born* in Israel after Israel's creation in 1948. He then is the "firstborn child" *birthed of the Hebrew Nation*, or God's firstborn son according to Exodus 4:22, to be the Israelis leader. Clearly, the status of being the "firstborn" Israeli leader will enhance Netanyahu's acceptance as *High Priest* after the *order* of Melchizedek, the leader of Jerusalem.

Let's continue to look at the double meaning of firstborn and how the *priestly heritage* was passed down through the lineage. Again there is the firstborn of the flesh, or of the womb, and then there is the firstborn of the Spirit, or children of God. Isaac was the firstborn of the Spirit, but he was not the firstborn child. His brother Ishmael was the firstborn son. In time, Isaac then had his two children, Esau and Jacob. Esau being the firstborn to open the womb should have received the covenant promises. God was going to raise up a great nation, a holy nation, and kingdom of priests. It should have been that this nation of priests came from the twelve sons/tribes of Esau and not the twelve tribes of Jacob. However, Esau, sold his birthright to Jacob because he did not value the things of God. In both of these cases, the younger sons, Isaac and Jacob, received the birthright.

Now this is quite ironic because it is contrary to the Word of God according to Deuteronomy 21:15-17:

15 If a man have two wives, one beloved, and another hated, and they have born him children, both the beloved and the hated; and if the firstborn son be hers that was hated:

16 Then it shall be, when he maketh his sons to inherit that which he hath, that he may not make the son of the beloved firstborn before the son of the hated, which is indeed the firstborn:

17 But he shall acknowledge the son of the hated for the firstborn, by giving him a double portion of all that he

hath: for he is the beginning of his strength; the right of the firstborn is his.

Here the Word specifically *forbids* "*man*" from setting aside the rights of the firstborn and **giving it to a younger son** from a better-loved wife. However, it was by the hand of "God" and not the hand of "man" that in both cases the younger child received the promise. God was working this out for *His purpose*. For example, when Jacob, the younger son of Isaac, had tricked his father into receiving the blessing, Isaac simply stated, " . . . yea, and he *shall* be blessed" (Genesis 27:33). This key verse tells us Isaac realized **God** had done this and not man. Notice Isaac did not try to change what had happened.

Later on in life Jacob then had children, and his firstborn son Rueben did not receive the birthright. Joseph, *his younger son by a better loved wife*, indirectly received the birthright through his two sons, Manasseh and Ephraim. Joseph then expected his firstborn son Manasseh to receive more; only to his dismay, the younger son was put before Manasseh. Angrily, Joseph told his father Jacob he was making a mistake. Joseph thought this because his father was aged and his eyesight was poor. Jacob however, quickly informed Joseph that he knew exactly what he was doing. Jacob told his son, " . . . **God make thee** as Ephraim and as Manasseh: and he set Ephraim before Manasseh" (Gen. 48:20). God was working this out for *His purpose*. The firstborn of the womb, concerning this particular lineage, was never really first. He never received all that God had intended for him, and this act can be distinctly traced going all the way back to Adam.

Romans 5:13-14 states, "For until the law sin was in the world: but sin is not imputed [assigned (2)] when there is no law. **Nevertheless death reigned from Adam to Moses, even over them that had not sinned after the similitude of Adam's transgression, who is the figure of him that was to come.*" I Corinthians 15:45 informs us that Adam was the "*figure*" of Jesus Christ. Jesus Christ is a *LEADER AND PRIEST* with total dominion. God, in Gen. ch. 1, blessed the "first" man, Adam, with all the earth and made him in **"His own image."**

86

Adam, in the figure and image of God, was then a leader and priest with total dominion over all the earth.

Nevertheless, death reigned from Adam to Moses. Adam had made a conscious decision to disobey God. The Bible says he was not deceived. God's Word was of no effect to him. So, he was cut off and kicked out of the Garden of Eden. *Because of Adam's sin, every firstborn man from Adam to Moses who like Adam was supposed to be a leader and a priest, made in God's own image, was cut off from having that position.* Death coming to the firstborn man was imminent; it did not matter whether or not these men sinned after the similitude of Adam. The leadership and priesthood were always passed to a second man.

This occurred because "(v. 47) [t]he first man is of the earth, earthy: the second man is the Lord from heaven. (v. 48) As is the earthy, such are they also that are earthy: and as is the heavenly, such are they also that are heavenly" (I Corinthians 15:47-48). The same chapter states there must first be a natural body and *afterwards* a spiritual body. First there was Adam, who was made of a living soul, and then the last Adam, Jesus Christ, who was made of a quickening spirit. *It was not possible for the seed of righteousness or the priesthood to be passed through the firstborn of the womb, which is of the flesh. *That spiritual seed had to be passed on to a second man and follow "due order"* (I Corinthians 15:22, 23). Remember there is the firstborn of the earth, or of the flesh, and **then** there is the firstborn of the Spirit, or of heaven, thereby giving 'firstborn' a double meaning.

The double meaning to the term firstborn truly manifests itself when looking at the pattern found among the *Israeli leaders* from Adam to Moses. The Bible gives us an account for these leaders who never inherited their firstborn rights: Adam, Cain, Ishmael, Esau, Rueben and Manasseh. Adam, the first to be cut off from the priesthood, had his first son named Cain, who followed in his father's footsteps. The Bible speaks of them both as *tillers of the ground*. They were earthy and not heavenly minded. Cain displeased God when he brought the fruit of the ground as an offering unto the Lord; he then became known as a vagabond. Cain's *younger* brother Abel pleased God because he brought the *"firstling"* of his flock as an offering unto the Lord. The Bible called him a "keeper of sheep."

The next given account of a "firstborn" son to be cut off from the priesthood was Ishmael. Ishmael, Abram or Abraham's first son, did not do anything wrong. *He "had not sinned after the similitude of Adam"*; nevertheless, he did not receive any rights of the firstborn. God's delay of Abraham's promised conception was long enough that Sarah, Abraham's wife, became tired of waiting for the promise. The Lord knew before it happened that Sarah would entice Abraham into having his son Ishmael with the bondwoman. The seed of righteousness would then be passed on through Isaac the second son, Abraham and Sarah's child.

The progression continues with Isaac. He had two children, as was mentioned earlier, and Jacob the youngest received the birthright. Romans chapter 9:7-8, 10-14, 17-18, 20-21 states,

> (v. 7) Neither, because they are the seed of Abraham, are they all children: but, In Isaac [the second man] shall thy seed be called. (v. 8) That is, They which are the children of the flesh, these are not the children of God: but the children of the promise are counted for the seed . . . . (v. 10) ***And not only this***; but when Rebecca also had conceived by one, even by our father Isaac; (v. 11) (For the children being not yet born, *neither having done any good or evil, that the purpose of God according* to *election* might stand, *not of works*, but of him that calleth;) (v. 12) It was said unto her, ***The elder shall serve the younger***. [Again, the second man was chosen.] (v. 13) As it is written, **Jacob have I loved**, but **Esau have I hated**. (v. 14) What shall we say then? Is there unrighteousness with God? God forbid . . . . (v. 17) For the scripture saith unto **Pharaoh** [Egypt's leader], Even for this **same purpose** have I raised thee up, that I might shew my power in thee, and that my name might be declared throughout all the earth. (v. 18) Therefore hath he mercy on whom he will have mercy, and whom he will he hardeneth . . . . (v. 20) Shall the thing formed say to him that formed it, *Why hast*

thou made me thus? (v. 21) Hath not the potter power over the clay, of the same lump to make one vessel unto honour, and another unto dishonour?

Examine these verses closely. Notice that the boys had not been born yet; they had not done any "work," **good** or **evil**. Yet God had a plan. He had a **PURPOSE** or intent. *Special note: the word "purpose" in this scripture means *to place before, i.e., (for oneself)* (3). Because of Adam's transgression, God was *placing* the second man, who, like Himself, would be of a heavenly nature *before* the first man which mirrored Adam, an earthy nature. God "loved" Jacob, the second man, because He knew Jacob would carry the seed of righteousness. God told Rebekah before the boys' birth the younger would be put before the elder. She took it upon herself to *work* with Jacob to steal a birthright already promised to the younger son.

Within the same breath God stated, "Esau have I hated." Esau, being the firstborn of the flesh, was predestined to be cut off from the priesthood. Remember that Esau was not even born yet. He had not done any good or *evil*. So, when the very God of heaven looked down and said I hate him, what He hated was what Esau represented. This firstborn child was merely a reflection of past leaders as well as future ones. For example, the identity of the ten Arab kings, that are part of the beast in Rev. 17:12, can be found through a study of Esau.

Esau, like the first leader Adam, chose to make a conscious decision to leave God. In Hebrews chapter 12, Esau was called profane because he sold his *birthright* for one morsel of meat. Because of this, verse 17 states, " . . . he found no place of repentance, though he sought it carefully with tears." **The very next time we see in the Word of God a person in a state of being irrecoverable is with the beast in Rev. ch. 14.** Revelation 14:9-11 portrays a place of hopelessness, a place of no repentance:

> (v. 9) If any man worship the beast and his image, and receive his mark in his forehead, or in his hand, (v. 10) The same shall drink of the wine of the wrath of God, which is poured out without mixture into the cup of his indignation; and he shall be tormented with fire and

brimstone in the presence of the holy angels, and in the presence of the Lamb: (v. 11) And the smoke of their torment ascendeth up *for ever and ever*: and they have no rest day nor night, who worship the beast and his image, and whosoever receiveth the mark of his name.

Today is the day for you to make a final decision. In giving away *your right to receive* the birthright, you will have made a covenant with the enemy, which automatically places you in a state of no repentance. Like Esau, you will be lost *forever*; and people, I am not just talking about 100 years, or 100,000 years, or a million years . . . it is forever!!! You will be tormented with fire and brimstone *forever!* Esau lost his birthright. He was a child of the flesh. Jacob, the second man, received the promise. Make your decision today, and follow after Jacob, a firstborn of the promise to receive a *heavenly nature*!

Concerning the firstborn leaders from Adam to Moses, God was intervening by raising them and putting them down to ultimately glorify His name through His people. God's name was going to "be declared throughout all the earth." Even Egypt's leader, Pharaoh, would have a part in this matter. *Remember the **same purpose** God had in mind between Pharaoh and Esau in Romans chapter 9:17? Now this same purpose begins to unravel. Death coming to the firstborn really began to manifest itself on the night of Passover in Egypt. *God, in order to accomplish His plan for the election*, hardened Pharaoh's heart. This then enabled Him to send a plague that would have slain every firstborn child in Egypt. Once again we see that *"all" firstborns would have been slain*; however, through this last plague God provided deliverance for His own people. *Like as with Esau*, God intended to cut off *all* the firstborns of the flesh.

After the Lord brought the people out of Egypt and into the wilderness, He then told Moses, "Sanctify unto me all the firstborn, **whatsoever** openeth the womb among the children of Israel . . . it is mine" (Exodus 13:2). Unlike before, there would now be a *body of firstborn sons* who would act out the role of both political and spiritual forms of government. This body of sons would now maintain the roles of both ruler and priests.

Exodus 13:11-13 continues,

> (v. 11) And it shall be ***when the LORD shall bring thee
> into the land of the Canaanites***, as he sware unto thee and
> to thy fathers, ***and shall give it thee***, (v. 12) That thou shalt
> set apart unto the LORD all that openeth the matrix, and
> every firstling that cometh of a beast which thou hast; the
> males shall be the LORD'S. (v. 13) And every firstling of
> an ass thou shalt redeem with a lamb; and if thou wilt not
> redeem it, then thou shalt break his neck: and all the
> firstborn of man among thy children shalt thou ***redeem.***

Again, all firstborn men had to be *redeemed.* God, in all of His
glory, was working this out "according to the election." Keep in
mind, Exodus 13:11, 12, informs us that this ordinance of
redeeming the firstborn would take place when the Jewish
people entered into their Promised Land. Later on, we will see
how this prophetically fits into the picture of the last days.

Continuing on, the phenomenon occurs again in the
wilderness of Sinai. In Exodus 19:3-6, Moses went up unto God
and the Lord called out to Moses from the mount renewing the
Abrahamic Covenant. God told Moses to relay the message that
if the Israelis kept God's covenant He would make Israel a holy
nation and kingdom of priests. God spoke of His
commandments in Exodus chapter 20. He said, "(v. 2) I am the
LORD thy God . . . . (v. 3) Thou shalt have no other gods before
me. (v. 4) Thou shalt not make unto thee any graven image, or
any likeness of any thing that is in heaven above, or that is in the
earth beneath . . . . (v. 5) Thou shalt not bow down thyself to
them, nor serve them: for I the LORD thy God am a jealous
God."

Then in Exodus chapter 32, we read that while Moses was
on the mount receiving the commandments, the people had made
a calf (an image) and worshiped it. The Lord's anger waxed hot,
and He wanted to smite all the people. Moses, however,
changed God's mind by interceding for them. Afterwards,
Moses descended off the mount and approached the camp. He
saw the people dancing about the calf, and in a rage of anger, he
broke the tables of stone and shouted, **"Who is on the LORD'S
side?"** (Ex. 32:26). At that point, the Bible says that the entire

tribe of Levi gathered together and stepped over unto the Lord's side. The rest of the people who did not make the right choice were either killed later or had to be redeemed. God took the Levites, *the second man*, to perform the priestly duties (Num. 3:45). Again God chose the second man "that His name might be declared throughout all the earth." He did this because, first there must be a *natural* body, and then there will be a *spiritual* body.

The warning of not worshiping any other god still stands even unto this day, for Revelation 13:15 tells us there will be another image created. It will be made in the likeness of the beast or the god of this world. People are going to worship it just as they did in those days. Recall Revelation 14:9, 10: "(v. 9) If any man worship the beast and his image, and receive his mark in his forehead, or in his hand, (v. 10) The same shall drink of the wine of the wrath of God."

When we consider the children of God in the wilderness, it is a shame that all "(v. 1) were under the cloud, and all passed through the sea; (v. 2) And were all baptized" (I Cor. 10:1, 2). They ate spiritual food and drank living water; nevertheless, some were overthrown. The people made a great transgression of sin when they made an image and worshiped it. They had made a covenant with the devil. They had forgotten what the Lord had done for them. *Their experience brings us to our conclusion for the purpose of all of this*: I Corinthians 10:11 states, "Now all these things happened unto them for ensamples [**fashion, resemblance (4)**]: and they are written for our admonition [**warning (5)**], upon whom the **ends of the world are come**." God will fashion these last days to resemble the days in the wilderness. *We are to learn from their mistakes* and not follow in their footsteps.

Keeping a prophetic view of the past, recall Jeremiah 23:7, 8:

> (v. 7) Therefore, behold, the days come, saith the LORD, that they shall no more say, The LORD liveth, which brought up the children of Israel out of the land of Egypt; (v. 8) But, The LORD liveth, which brought up and which led the seed of the house of Israel out of the north country,

and from all countries whither I had driven them; ***and they shall dwell in their own land***.

In the modeling of Israel's beginning experience and the fulfillment of prophecy, God has brought the Hebrew Nation of Israel, **HIS FIRSTBORN SON (Ex. 4:22)**, *back into their Promised Land.* He has delivered them for a "second time" to make them an ensign for the Gentile nations (see Isaiah 11:11, 12, 16).

Born in Tel Aviv on October 21, 1949, Benjamin Netanyahu the "*FIRSTBORN* LEADER" OF THE HEBREW NATION will "claim" to be Israel's <u>King</u> and <u>High Priest</u> after the order of Melchizedek, leader of Jerusalem. Recall from page 83, Psalms 110:4, is a messianic psalm that teaches us that the leader or the ruler of the Hebrew Nation would be able to reflect in his person the role of a king as well as the role of a priest. Realize then the significance of Jerusalem's "chief leader" as he addresses Israel's Knesset: "I was *fortunate* to be the '***first*' among Israeli prime ministers to be '*born*' after the establishment of the state of Israel**. The torch has been passed unto us by the generation born with the founding of the state of Israel 1948." (6)

Following the footsteps of history, from Adam to Moses and then again in the wilderness, the **FIRSTBORN LEADER OF THE HEBREW NATION**, will once again be cut off from his position, along with all of those who follow after his authority. In finishing his speech, Netanyahu quotes from the Old Testament prophet Amos, "***AND I SHALL ESTABLISH FOR THEM DAVID'S FALLEN TABERNACLE***." Possessed by Satan, Netanyahu is going to establish a *throne* of authority, but it will not be God's throne. Realize that this is the day of decision!

WHO IS ON THE LORD'S SIDE???!!

Chapter 8
The Tabernacle

The *Revell Bible Dictionary* describes the tabernacle:
> [E]ach aspect of the [tabernacle's] <u>construction</u> has symbolic implications. Thus, Moses was told to be sure to construct it 'according to the pattern shown you on the mountain' (Ex. 25:40). The NT picks up this thought, saying that the tabernacle was "a copy and shadow of what is in heaven" (Heb. 8:5). (1)

God placed specific words within the verses of Ex. 26 to help excavate prophetic truths. The definitions of these selected words <u>*in order*</u> from verse to verse will construct the events that shall occur in our final days. The plan of the tabernacle "given on the mount" stood as a figuration of the last day events. The authenticity of the prophetic meaning to Ex. 26 is established when comparing it to Da. chapter 11.

Once in the wilderness, God instructed Moses to build a tabernacle so that He may dwell among the Israelites. This tabernacle was covered with eleven goat hair curtains. <u>*These eleven curtains are symbolic for one Jewish leader Benjamin Netanyahu, and ten Arab kings</u>.

> <u>Exodus 26:7</u> And thou shalt make *curtains of goats' hair* to be a covering upon the tabernacle: *eleven curtains* shalt thou make.

The Arabs, in ways similar to Moses' days, still use goat hair curtains to cover their tents, thereby protecting themselves from wet stormy weather. An example of this custom was found in an article taken from the *St. Petersburg Times*. The article describes a young Arab girl, "With only a *goat hair curtain protecting* her from the world." (2)

Goat's hair, used to provide security, has always been and still is characteristic of the Arab world. This usage can be distinctly traced all the way back to Genesis chapter 27. Here, we find the allegory of Esau and Jacob presenting a prophetic pattern found in the construction of the tabernacle. Jacob, later named "Israel," *deceitfully* put on the skins of two kid goats to represent Esau, the Arabs of today! JACOB, OR ISRAEL, PUT ON GOAT'S HAIR TO BECOME AN ARAB! We can relate this directly to what is occurring today through a study of *the tabernacle which shadows the nation of Israel* (Isaiah 54:1-5; Hebrews 9:8, 9).

Providing **"SECURITY" TO THE TABERNACLE FROM STORMY WEATHER**, the covering of the *eleven goat hair curtains* is symbolic of the peace treaty signings between the Arabs and the Jews. Hence, the Arabs tell the Israelis, "We will provide '*security*' and protect you from the *stormy weather, if you will only partake of our offer.*" And so the Jewish community in wanting to fulfill its desire for *peace and security,* have given away their birthright, their livelihood. Israel, like Jacob, has "put on" or covered itself with Arab garments. Yet this deal shall not prosper, for it is only an act of *deception.* Jeremiah 6:14 unveils the mask stating, "They have healed also the hurt of the daughter of my people slightly, saying, Peace, peace; *when there is no peace.*" From the outside, the tabernacle *covered by the eleven goat hair curtains* was not a pretty site to behold, and even more ugly to the eye is the facade this peace treaty creates!

Within Exodus 26:7, there is another underlying message. Specifically, this verse states there are *eleven* goat hair curtains covering the tabernacle. These eleven goat hair curtains are symbolic for one Jewish leader coupled together with ten Arab kings. Recall in Genesis 27, Jacob, symbolic for the Antichrist before he received his name change, became Esau to receive the spiritual blessing, and it was all an act of deception. The Antichrist headed on the same course will put on Arab garments to deceive and receive his spiritual blessing.

Exodus 26:8 The length of one curtain shall be thirty cubits, and the breadth of one curtain four cubits: and the eleven curtains shall be all of one *measure.*

96

Supporting Definitions:

1) <u>Measure</u> – portion (a part esp. that allotted to a person
   (3)), vestment (a "garment" or robe, esp. one worn by a
   "clergyman" (4)) (5).

*<u>*So measure means a "garment" worn by a priest*</u>. *Priestly
garments* are discussed in Exodus 29; here are the Hebrew
definitions for both of these words:

    a) <u>priest</u> - an acting priest (although a layman):- chief
       ruler (6).

    b) <u>garments</u> – treachery (betrayal of trust (7)); pillage
       (plunder (8) [rob or take property by force or fraud
       (9)]) (10).

Also note, in Exodus 29, the priest and his garments had to
be hollowed or made clean. *They were dirty instruments*
before the Lord prior to the cleaning (Exodus 29:21).

The eleven curtains shall (future) be "all of one" *measure*.
These eleven men, wearing all the same **garments**, shall unite
and become one for a common purpose or goal. Revelation
17:12 and 13 explains these men: "(v. 12) . . . *ten kings* . . .
receive power . . . with the *beast* [making eleven]. (v. 13) These
have <u>one mind</u>, and shall give their power and strength unto the
beast." Benjamin Netanyahu, Israel's *chief ruler*, will claim to
be the *high priest* when he calls himself the "I AM." Wearing
the *garments of betrayal*, he will *pillage* Israel's property from
before her. (Note: the Israeli authorities have already tried to
indict Israel's *chief ruler*, Benjamin Netanyahu, on breach of
trust and *fraud* charges concerning the Hebron settlement.)

<u>Exodus 26:9-10</u> (v. 9) And thou shalt couple five curtains
    by themselves, and six *curtains* by themselves, and shalt
    double the *sixth curtain* in the *forefront* of the
    tabernacle. (v. 10) And thou shalt make fifty loops on
    the edge of the one curtain that is outmost in the
    coupling . . . .

Supporting Definitions:

1) <u>double</u> – double (two-fold (11)) (12).
2) <u>curtain / curtains</u> - *EVIL MAN*, associate selves [by mistake for], to tend a flock, to rule, to associate with (as a friend): - devour, evil entreat (13).
3) <u>forefront</u> - the face (as the part that turns); front (leading position (14)) (15).
4) <u>loops</u> - to fold back (16).
5) <u>edge</u> - through the idea of termination; the lip (as a natural boundary); scatter (17).
6) <u>outmost</u> - to spend the harvest season; harvest (as the crop), whether the product (grain or fruit) (18).
7) <u>coupling</u> - to join; specifically (by means of spells) (19).

From the above, we see the curtains, *evil men*, are not totally united yet; five curtains were joined together by themselves and the other six by themselves. The *sixth curtain* has had special attention drawn to it. This *evil man* is distinct from the other ten. He has been *"doubled"* at the forefront, or the *leading position* of the tabernacle. The sixth curtain represents Benjamin Netanyahu, and his being doubled at the forefront of the tabernacle means he has a *two-fold part.* *Bibi has a *face that turns both ways*. *<u>Not only is he the leader of Israel, but he shall also be the leader of the ten Arab kings.</u>

Again, <u>curtain means evil man</u>, assoc. selves [by mistake for] to tend a flock, to rule, to associate with (as a friend):- devour, evil entreat. Benjamin Netanyahu as the *"shepherd of the flock,"* will *associate* himself *as a friend to Israel.* Many of the Jews will rally behind Benjamin Netanyahu; yet, he will *devour to evil entreat* them. He will "scatter among them the prey, and spoil, and riches" (Daniel 11:24). It appears Bibi will decrease Israel's *natural boundaries*, which he has already, and spend the *harvest season.* With Satan at the helm, all of this will be done by *"means of spells."*

*Special Note: Exodus 26:11-15, 17, correlates perfectly with Daniel 11:30, 31, 33.

Exodus 26:11   And thou shalt make fifty *taches of brass*, and put the taches into the loops, and *couple* the tent together, that it may be one.

Supporting Definitions:

1) taches - to protrude (project (20) [scheme, to cause (21)]) (22).
2) brass - Cypress, part of the Grecian Empire.
3) couple - to join, specifically (by means of spells) (23).

Here the taches of "brass" are responsible for bringing the curtains or men together. In Chapter 10 of this book I discuss how Nebuchadnezzar's image will rise and walk again to become the beast in this last day. Recall from pg. 56, the stomach and thighs of **brass** in Nebuchadnezzar's image symbolized the *Grecian Empire*. In like manner, the taches of *brass* in this verse are symbolic for the *Greek* Island of Cyprus. *Cyprus*, in stirring up trouble, will push Benjamin Netanyahu's hand *causing* the Antichrist and the Arabs to become one; compare Daniel 11:30-31 on pgs. 45-46. Once again in the Word of God, this same theme appears in Daniel 2:45. There the brass is strategically placed in between the iron (Arabs) and the clay (Jews), displaying how it shall unite the two. All of this will be done through *means of spells*. The next two verses in Exodus, 12 and 13, coincide perfectly with what I have stated.

Exodus 26:12   And the *remnant* that remaineth of the curtains of the tent, the *half curtain* that remaineth, shall hang over the *backside* of the *tabernacle*.

Supporting Definitions:

1) remnant - to stretch self (24).
2) half - *to divide, x live out half, reach to the midst* (25).
3) curtain - to be broken up (with any violent action), be grievous (26).

99

4) backside - *after (-ward)*, hereafter (27).
5) tabernacle - a residence (including a shepherd's hut, the lair [a resting place of a wild animal (28)] of animals, fig. the grave) (29).

Verse 11 told us these men will come together. They will become "one." Once that happens, then devastation will occur. When pushed by Cyprus, Benjamin Netanyahu will become *grievous*, making his final decision of betrayal. When the Prime Minister signed the Hebron deal, I believe he confirmed the covenant of Daniel 9:27, thus, beginning the final seven-year period. As the half curtain suggests, Benjamin Netanyahu will *divide* that seven-year period and *live out half*. The first three and a half-year period, he will ascend through peace and diplomacy. Suddenly, as he *reaches to the midst*, or the middle of a seven-year period, Netanyahu and the other men/curtains will *break up the tabernacle with a violent action*. In other words, in the middle of this seven-year period, Benjamin Netanyahu will sit in the temple of God claiming to be God. *Afterward*, the *tabernacle* shall become a *resting-place of wild animals, a grave*. Jesus told us in Matthew 24:15, 16 when the man of sin, stands in the holy place, or in the temple, then those that are in Judea need to FLEE. Verse 21 says, "For then shall be great tribulation, such as was not since the beginning of the world to this time, no, nor ever shall be." We see tribulation and those fleeing from it in the next two verses.

Exodus 26:13   And a *cubit* on the one side, and a cubit on the other side of that which remaineth in the length of the curtains of the tent, it shall hang over the sides of the tabernacle *on this side* and *on that side*, to *cover* it.

Supporting Definitions:

1) cubit - fore-arm [to prepare in advance for a conflict (30)] (31).
2) side - to sidle (to move in a furtive (32) [or secret (33)] manner) off; adversary (34).

100

3) cover - (flee to) hide (35).

In betraying his country, Netanyahu together with the Arabs will have **prepared in advance for this conflict**. Suddenly, with everything done in **secret action**, Jerusalem will be encompassed by her adversary. And many shall **FLEE to hide**. (See also Luke 21:20-24.)

> Exodus 26:14   And thou shalt make a *covering* for the tent of *rams' skins* dyed red, and a covering above of *badgers' skins*.

Supporting Definitions:

1) covering - be covered with flesh, time appointed, **COVERED, I.E. A THRONE** (as canopied):- **THRONE** (36).
2) rams' - chief (politically) (37).
3) skins - skin (as naked) (38).
4) badgers' skins - ". . . goats' skins (RSV) . . . " (39).

Remember that Jacob put on goats' skins to become Esau, the Arabs of today.
*Special Note: Each time there is another article applied to the tabernacle, it is symbolic of some future event that will occur in our last days.

After the tent is coupled together, or these eleven men unite to desecrate the tabernacle, then we see the ram and goat skins *applied to their lives*. Meaning, once Benjamin Netanyahu, (the **chief "politically")**, unites with the Arabs (or *goats skins),* **then** their **nakedness** will be exposed. Like as with Judas, the apostles did not realize whom the trader was until *they saw him coming with the multitude to take Jesus*. The conspiracy will be in the open once these men come with force and place the abomination that maketh desolate.
At the *appointed time*, Satan veiled in *flesh*, will *"cover a throne"* in the temple of God. II Thes. 2:4 states, " . . . he as

God *sitteth* in the temple of God." In Greek, sitteth means *to sit down*, *"covered"* (40). What is he going to sit down on? What is he going to cover. . . . .a throne! According to *Revell Bible Dictionary*, " . . . one function of the king was judicial, the image of a king *taking his throne* may suggest judgment" (41). This dictionary also explains that "judgment [i]n the OT (means) a condemnation or punishment decreed by a ruler" (42). It only stands to follow, when Benjamin Netanyahu *takes a throne*, judicial punishment should occur, and this becomes evident in the next verse.

Exodus 26:15, 17 (v. 15) And thou shalt make *boards* for the tabernacle of *shittim wood standing* up . . . . (v. 17) Two *tenons* shall there be in one board.

Supporting Definitions:

1) boards - to split off (43).
2) shittim - to flog, whip (44).
3) wood - to close (the eyes):- shut (45).
4) standing - be employed (46).
5) tenons - a hand (the open one) (47).

From these verses, it appears there are two types of people. Once the conflict begins, these men will *split off*. One man will *flog* the victims, while the other man will *close his eyes* to the abuse. This is exactly what happened to Jesus Christ. The Romans, under the influence of the Jews, imposed a double sentence on Christ that under Jewish law was unlawful. *Search for Truth* explains: "Jewish law specified that no 'prolonged death' might be inflicted and that a criminal condemned to death must not also be scourged" (48) or flogged (49). While the Romans unlawfully flogged and crucified the Lord, the Jewish people *closed their eyes* to the crime. As history repeats itself, the ***RULERS OF ZION*** will again have an *open hand* to bribery.

Exodus 26:24 And they shall be coupled together *beneath*,

102

and they shall be coupled together above the *head* of it unto one *ring:* thus shall it be for them both; they shall be for the two corners.

Supporting Definitions:

1) beneath - underneath; [through the idea of a film over the eyes]; to blind, skin (as naked); be made naked (50).
2) head - (time, rank):- beginning, chief, ruler (51).
3) ring – a seal (pledge, to decide finally (52)), signet [derived from a sign (53), mark (54)] (55).

Controlled by Satan, the beast will now offer its mark. When the beast places this *mark underneath* the *skin*, the individual will *be made naked* before the Lord. Anyone who takes this mark under his or her skin will be *blind* to any truth concerning the Word of God. This mark will be a *pledge* to Satan. When the mark is offered, it will be a time of choice, a time for a final decision. The mark that will be offered to people will center "around" the *head* of the Hebrew Nation, Benjamin Netanyahu; thus, they shall be coupled together beneath and above the "*head*" into one ring. Revelation 13:17, 18 reminds us, "(v. 17) And that no man might buy or sell, save he that had the *mark*, or the *name* of the beast, or the *number* of his name. (v. 18) Here is wisdom. Let him that hath understanding *count the number* of the beast: for it is the number of a man; and his number is Six hundred threescore and six" (666).

Think about these definitions:
1) mark - to describe (56).
2) name – authority (57).
3) number – count (58) (to name (59)); number (as reckoned up) number, keep in suspense; by Heb. [comp. 5375] to expiate sin (60). (Reckon means to regard as being) (61).

**In the last day, the *mark* given will *describe* the *name* or *authority* given to a man. One could also say the mark, or *number (666)*, will describe the day in which he was *regarded as being* an authority.

There are three significant, yet different, periods of time, which describe Benjamin Netanyahu being regarded as an authority. First of all, the final results of Israel's election, which confirmed Benjamin Netanyahu as the country's new Prime Minister, came in on a Friday night, just before the Jewish Sabbath. Benjamin Netanyahu was regarded as being Israel's Prime Minister on the **SIXTH DAY** of the week. Once the news was announced, Bibi then had the right, or the *"authority,"* to name his 18-member cabinet. Secondly, Netanyahu was not sworn in to receive his *authority* to the nation until the **SIXTH MONTH** of June; Shimon Peres held the office until then. Thirdly, he began to "rule and reign" in the **SIXTH YEAR** or 199**6**. When we compute or count the days in which Bibi was named as Israel's leader, we come up with the sixth day of the sixth month of the sixth year! **THE NUMBER TO HIS NAME, OR WHEN HE RECEIVED HIS AUTHORITY, IS 666!!!**

__The tabernacle in the wilderness was a prophetic picture of the last day events__. It was a foreshadowing of both good and evil things to come. II Thess. 2:4 tells us the Antichrist will sit in the temple of God showing himself to be God and demanding the worship of the people. *__THOSE WHO SERVE GOD WILL KNOW NOT TO WORSHIP AT THIS TEMPLE IN JERUSALEM, FOR__*:

1) John 4:19-24: (v. 19) The woman saith unto him [Jesus] . . . (v. 20) [o]ur fathers worshipped in this mountain; and ye say, that in Jerusalem is the place where men ought to worship. (v. 21) Jesus saith unto her, *Woman, believe me, the hour cometh, when ye shall neither in this mountain, nor yet at Jerusalem, worship the Father.* (v. 22) Ye worship ye know not what (he was telling her she did not have the truth): we know what we worship; for salvation is of the Jews. (v. 23) But the hour cometh, and **NOW IS**, when the true worshippers shall worship the Father in spirit and in "truth" . . . . (v. 24) God is a Spirit: and they

that worship him must worship him in spirit and in truth.

2) Acts 17:24: **_GOD_** that made the world and all things therein . . . **_DWELLETH NOT IN TEMPLES_** made with hands.

3) Hebrews 9:11: . . . Christ being come an high priest of good things to come, by a greater and more perfect tabernacle, not made with hands, that is to say, not of this building.

Under the law the Jews, at the temple, would offer up the blood of bulls and goats for the atonement of one's sins. Yet, it was impossible for this offering unto God to ever cleanse anyone. Jesus Christ, the sinless sacrifice came to the earth to become our once sacrificial offering that we might become the sons of God through our obedience unto the Lord (Heb. 5:9). Referring to the endtime, the Word states in II Thess. ch. 2:4, "he [the Antichrist] as God sitteth in the _temple of God_, showing himself that he is God." Understand, the temple of God, which the Antichrist will sit in, is it of God or is it of man? ****It is of God, _ONLY_ in the sense that God is allowing it in the fulfillment of prophecy!**

Chapter 9
The Hidden Secret

"(v. 20) . . . Blessed be the name of God for ever and ever: for wisdom and might are his: (v. 21) And he changeth the times and the seasons: **he removeth kings, and setteth up kings**: he giveth wisdom unto the wise, and knowledge to them that know understanding: (v. 22) **He revealeth the deep and secret things**: he knoweth what is in the darkness, and the light dwelleth with him" -- Daniel 2:20-22.

As these words from Daniel testify, only God reveals the secret things. We will know His greatness and observe His mighty hand as we study the following scriptures taken from Daniel chapters 2, 4, 5, 7 and Revelation chapters 12, 13, 14, 17. It will become very apparent just how tightly woven these chapters are by the end of the next two studies.

As stated in the scripture, God brings up kings and puts them down. The book of Daniel speaks particularly of two kings who presided over the Babylonian Empire, and I would like to discuss these kings. However, before we look at these two rulers and how they relate to endtime prophecy, I would like to glance quickly at the empire they ruled from.

Babylon, earlier named Babel, was an ungodly unholy city. It symbolized human pride and rebellion against God. Explanations from two Bible dictionaries will help us understand this concept: First, "The name is derived by the Hebrews from the root bālal ('to confound') and has reference to the confusion of tongues at the Tower (Genesis 11:9). Thus the biblical writer refutes any God-honoring connotation of the name" (1). Second, "As predicted in Isa. 13:19, 20, Babylon ultimately became a completely deserted site" (2). However, "Mystery" Babylon is spoken of in the book of Revelation. This kingdom represents mankind and its achievements without respect to God. The religious twist to it is seen in Revelation 17, and man's materialistic achievements are noted in Revelation 18. To understand the hidden secret of "Mystery" Babylon, we must begin with a study of Daniel and the other two kings who were to rule from the Babylonian Empire.

To begin with, look at King Nebuchadnezzar. In the third year of his reign, God allowed Nebuchadnezzar to besiege Jerusalem, burn the house of God down to the ground and take the **vessels** of the house of God back to Babylon to put them in the house of his god. Nebuchadnezzar, the Bible says, was a man who had exalted himself. He thought he could do all things and without God. Allowing his pride to get in the way, he believed he had created the kingdom with his own hands. His arrogant attitude soon got him into trouble as God pronounced judgment on him, turning him into a *beast*. Nebuchadnezzar was made to eat grass as oxen for seven years until he finally realized the mighty God from heaven ruled.

Relating this to our day, Yitzhak Rabin was another Nebuchadnezzar. God allowed Rabin to touch the land, which, like the vessels, was put aside for *God's service*. It was all part of God's unfolding plan for Jerusalem. Rabin, a leader who took God out of the picture, *was going to build a kingdom all on his own*. Because the power was in his hands, the former Israeli Prime Minister touched the *land* and surrendered it for peace. Like Nebuchadnezzar, Rabin was brought down, and many people had seen this as God's hand fulfilling prophecy.

The second man to form the triangular formation was Belshazzar. Understand Nebuchadnezzar did wrong when he took the vessels and placed them in the house of his god. However, Belshazzar as his successor, did worse when he took the "(v. 2) . . . vessels which his father Nebucadnezzar had taken out of the temple which was in Jerusalem . . . (v. 3) [and] drank in them" (Da. 5:2, 3). Daniel 5:22 states, "And thou his son, O Belshazzar, hast not humbled thine heart, **though thou knewest all this**." Belshazzar was in a worse position than Nebuchadnezzar, whose heart was lifted up, because Belshazzar had knowledge of God's judgment upon Nebuchadnezzar. Yet, Belshazzar not only took the vessels, he drank from them as well. He *worshiped other gods* with the vessels and within that same hour a hand appeared, which brought forth a message upon the wall:

"MENE, MENE, TEKEL, UPHARSIN" -- Da. 5:25. "These words are names of Babylonian weights or coins. <u>Each coin has a lesser value than the preceding</u>. In English, the saying might be, 'Dollar, dollar, quarter, dime'" (3).

In essence, these coins are an illustration of the men. Each ruler has a lesser value than his predecessor.

Shaken by the writing upon the wall, the king called for Daniel the prophet. Belshazzar told Daniel,

(v. 16) And I have heard of thee, that thou canst make interpretations, and dissolve doubts: now if thou canst read the writing, and make known to me the interpretation thereof, thou shalt be clothed with **scarlet**, and have a chain of gold about thy neck, and shalt be the third ruler in the kingdom. [The beast is scarlet in color in Rev.17:3.] (v. 17) ***Then Daniel answered and said before the king, Let thy gifts be to thyself, and give thy rewards to another***; yet I will read the writing unto the king, and make known to him the interpretation . . . . (v. 25) And this is the writing that was written, **MENE, MENE, TEKEL, UPHARSIN** . . . . (v. 26) **MENE; God hath numbered thy kingdom, and finished it**. (v. 27) **TEKEL; Thou art weighed in the balances, and art found wanting**. (v. 28) <u>**PERES**</u> . . ." (Daniel 5:16, 17, 25-28).

Notice how UPHARSIN is not mentioned in the interpretation Daniel gave to Belshazzar; "Peres" is there instead. God certainly did take care of Shimon Peres, for at the age of 72, with three fatal attempts for the Prime Minister's position, *he is finished*. He was voted out of office. Peres' name being interpreted in Hebrew means to divide (4). Peres did as his name suggests; he "divided the kingdom" and gave it to the enemy. It was God's Word being fulfilled.

*****Belshazzar** succeeded **Nebuchadnezzar**, like *Peres* succeeded **Rabin**. Shadowed in the story of Belshazzar, we find the story of Peres. The word *Peres* appearing in the message God sent to Belshazzar is no coincidence. God saw into the future the ungodly acts of Rabin and Peres. God knew Peres would worsen the condition before him. Peres was a *raiser of taxes* (pgs. 26-27). He was known as the architect of the covenant, the peace treaty between the Arabs and the Jews. He helped to coerce Rabin into taking a step toward peace. "MENE, MENE, TEKEL, UPHARSIN . . . DOLLAR, DOLLAR, QUARTER, DIME?"

The third ruler completing the triangle was Daniel, *God's chosen*. Looking at Daniel in this position will unveil the hidden secret that will help us to understand the formation of the beast. Daniel received this position from giving Belshazzar the interpretation of the writing that appeared upon the wall. Once Daniel had given the interpretation, the Bible says in Daniel 5:29, " . . . and they clothed Daniel with scarlet, and put a chain of gold about his neck, and made a proclamation concerning him, that **he should be the *third ruler* in the kingdom**."

Daniel, a Jew and God's chosen vessel, put on the garments of a Babylonian ruler. Imagine that, one of God's chosen was to become the "third ruler" of Babylon, an ungodly unholy nation that was doomed to destruction. Ask yourself, why would Daniel do this? Why would he allow the king to make him the third ruler over Babylon? Remember, Daniel had told Belshazzar, just prior to giving the interpretation, to give his rewards to *another* (Da. 5:17). Why would Daniel then suddenly change his mind? Here was a *man of God*, who maintained a purpose in his heart not to eat of the king's meat because it would defile his body (Dan.1:8).

We see this same nobility in Daniel's companions and servants of the most High, Shadrach, Meshach and Abednego. These men were "commanded" by Nebuchadnezzar to bow down and worship before the king's golden image. If they refused, they would be thrown into the burning fiery furnace. Nevertheless, these wise men would not bow down because God's servants knew they had another "option"! They told the king *God was able* to deliver them from the fiery furnace; yet, if He chose not to, they still would not bow. No doubt, these men of God knew they had a way of escape. They knew God was able to deliver them, and Daniel knew this as well.

Daniel did not have to wear the garments of a king to an

ungodly unholy nation. Undoubtedly, Daniel, a great man of God, would have trusted in the Lord to deliver him out of the hands of Belshazzar the king. Daniel understood there was another "*option*" before putting on the unholy garments and defiling himself. Still, there was a purpose for Daniel's actions. He wore the garments *as a symbolic gesture only*. God, through Daniel's actions, was showing us who would be the third ruler of this man-made kingdom. "Mystery Babylon" was going to be headed by a Jew, one of God's chosen! Benjamin Netanyahu is that Jew. Netanyahu succeeded "Peres," like Daniel succeeded "Belshazzar." Daniel put on the ungodly garments knowing God would protect him from actually taking that position. Hence, he had already told Belshazzar the kingdom was going to be given into the enemies' hands! Sure enough in that *same night*, Darius the Median conquered Babylon and took over the kingdom.

Chapter 10
The Beast

Have you wondered lately who the next world super power will be? Stop wondering; the answer is in Daniel chapter 2. The story began with King Nebuchadnezzar of Babylon who had a dream that troubled his spirit. Unable to recall it, he called for the magicians and the astrologers to reveal the dream unto him. However, when they were unable to do so, the king issued a decree to slay all the wise men in the area. Now when the prophet Daniel had heard this, he promised to reveal the dream to the king. After receiving the answer from God, Daniel went before the king and said,

> (v. 31) Thou, O king, sawest, and behold a great image. This great image, whose brightness was excellent, stood before thee; and the form thereof was terrible. (v. 32) This image's head was of fine gold, his breast and his arms of silver, his belly and his thighs of brass, (v. 33) His legs of iron, his feet part of iron and part of clay. (v. 34) Thou sawest till that a stone [referring to Jesus Christ, see Matthew 16:18 and Isaiah 28:16] was cut out without hands, which smote the image upon his feet that were of iron and clay, and brake them to pieces. (v. 35) Then was the iron, the clay, the brass, the silver, and the gold, broken to pieces together, and became like the chaff of the summer threshingfloors; and the wind carried them away, that no place was found for them: and the stone that smote the image became a great mountain, and filled the whole earth. (Daniel 2:31-35)

The image seen in Nebuchadnezzar's dream formed the body of a man. This body was divided into five subsequent parts representing *four past kingdoms* and *one future kingdom*. The anatomy of the man was described by the various uses of metals. *Each body part, containing metallic substance, was symbolic for a world empire:*

1) The **head** **of** **gold** represented **Babylon**, King Nebuchadnezzar being that head (Daniel 2:38).

2) The **chest and arms of silver** modeled the **Medo-Persian** kingdom, which superseded Babylon at the end of the Jews' 70 year captivity.
3) The **belly and thighs of brass** stood for the **Grecian Empire** headed by Alexander the Great around 334 B.C. Then, after his death the kingdom was divided among four generals.
4) The image's **legs of iron** represented **Rome**, which replaced Greece in their domination around 63 B.C. In 300 A.D. the Empire was divided into Eastern and Western Empires by Diocletion. Though the Roman Empire does not stand today, she still plays a major role in both of our world government and religion, even to this day.

Note: numbers 1-4 above were derived from the
Search for Truth Bible Study.

5) The **feet** of this image were made of **part of iron** and **part of clay**. Pages 56-58 teach these substances are symbolic for the **Eastern Roman Empire** and the so called **"religious" leaders in Israel**. Daniel 2:43 tells us both of these shall mingle themselves with the *seed of men*, the **Roman Catholic Church. The seed of men, represented by the Pope, is right now mingling itself with both the Arabs and the Jews!!**

*Study the meaning of the "seed of men." According to the *Revell Bible Dictionary*, seed "in Scripture stands for (1) a person's descendants (Gen. 12:7, KJV), and (2) specifically the Messiah, Jesus, the particular descendant in whom God's covenant promises to Abraham are fulfilled (Gal. 3:16). [J]esus compared his death to a seed which, planted in the ground, 'dies' as a separate entity, *but multiplies itself through the plant it generates* (Jn. 12:24)" (1). The *PLANT* that Jesus generated was the *GOSPEL*. When the seed in John 12:24 hit the ground and died, newness of life sprung forth. Now through *obeying the gospel* and following the example of Jesus Christ, we can become the seed of Abraham.

During the reign of Pope John 23rd, the Roman Catholic

Church proclaimed, "'**WE, THE _MOTHER CHURCH_**, are opening our arms to all of **OUR DAUGHTERS** (multiplied herself like a seed) to return home . . . . We trust that, with the approach of the year 2000, Jerusalem will become the city of peace for the _entire world_ and that all the people will be able to meet there, <u>in particular the believers in the religions that find their _birthright_ in the faith of Abraham!</u>'" (2). The Pope is claiming to be of the seed of Abraham when in fact he is the seed (carnally (3); Dan. 2:43) of men. He claimed, in the newly released Catechism on pgs. 242-243, "'[t]he _**plan of salvation**_ also includes those who acknowledge the Creator, in the first place amongst whom are _the Muslims_; these profess to hold the faith of Abraham, and _together with us_ they adore the one, merciful God, mankind's judge on the last day'" (4).

The Pope here has generated a _**different plant**_, a different gospel when there is no other plan of salvation! He is showing unity with the Arabs who believe in Alah and not Jesus Christ. Yet, Jesus said in John 8:24, 27 that unless you believe He is the Father, you will _surely die_ in your sins. The Roman Catholic Church is also going to great lengths in mingling with the Jews. The Vatican just recently, on Dec. 1997, lit a Hanukkah candle under the Arch of Titus, built in celebration of the destruction of the Jews' second temple. The _seed of men_, represented by the Pope, is mingling with the <u>iron</u> and the <u>clay</u>.

The feet of this man, made of iron and clay (or Arabs and Jews), represent a last day kingdom. This kingdom in the near future _shall_ form and "carry" all of the other kingdoms, (Babylon, Medes-Persian, Greece, and the Roman Empire), right into Armageddon. One last time, Nebuchadnezzar's image will unite, stand and walk again in this last day. We know this because:

1) The image was in the form of a man, and you cannot separate a man's head from his feet.
2) In Daniel 2:35, the stone, Jesus Christ, smote the image's feet and then **"all"** the kingdoms came down **"together."**
3) <u>Daniel 2:44</u>: **"And in the days of these kings shall the**

115

God of heaven set up a kingdom, which shall never be destroyed: and the kingdom shall not be left to other people, but it shall break in pieces and consume **all "these" kingdoms**, and it shall stand for ever." *Revelation 17:12 refers to the ten men as having **"a"** (singular) *kingdom* in the future. Therefore, Daniel 2:44 is referring to *all* the kingdoms which make up Nebuchadnezzar's image as being destroyed and not just the <u>singular kingdom</u> of the image's feet.

    4) Daniel 2:45 states, "Forasmuch as thou sawest that the stone was cut out of the mountain without hands, and that it brake in pieces <u>the iron, the **brass**, the clay, the silver, and the gold</u>; the great God hath made known to the king what shall come to pass hereafter."

On three different occasions, in Daniel chapter 2, the kingdoms were described in a progressive manner, moving and creating the image either from head to foot or foot to head (see Da. 2:32-34, 35, 38-41). There is one exception, Da. 2:45, see #4 above. Here God changed the order in which the kingdoms were displayed. There is a reason for this, for God is a God of order. Instead of placing the brass between the silver and iron, **the Lord strategically placed the "brass" between the iron and the clay**: iron, being the Eastern Roman Empire (Arabs); brass, being the Grecian Empire; clay, being the Jewish Nation. *<u>God placed the Grecian Empire between the iron and the clay because in Daniel 11:30, the Greek Island of Chittim (Cyprus) will stir up trouble to cause the final thrust which will bring "together" the Arabs with the Jews.</u>

At the point of being pushed, the Jewish nation with Benjamin Netanyahu as their "guide" will forfeit the temple over into the Gentile or Arab hands. For in Daniel 11:31, as was explained earlier, Netanyahu makes his decision to return home with arms, and like Judas, he desecrates the temple of God. (*And do not forget, in the tabernacle God used taches of "**brass**" to unite the "11 goat hair curtains" -- see Exodus 26:11.) So it is in all three cases: Daniel 2:45, Daniel 11:30, and Exodus 26:11, the brass, symbolic for the Grecian Empire, shall bring together the Arabs and the Jews. God's Word is just awesome! Every intricate detail has its place!

Without question, the dream God gave Nebuchadnezzar was symbolic for a final kingdom which will try to rule this earth prior to the return of Jesus Christ. To confirm this, turn to Daniel chapter 7 of your Bible and study Daniel's night vision of the four beasts. Daniel chapter 7, in brief, tells us: 1) the first beast Daniel saw was like a lion, 2) the second beast was like a bear, 3) the third beast was like a leopard, 4) the fourth beast was described as having great iron teeth, and it had ten horns with a little horn that came up among them. Using Nebuchadnezzar's image as an outline will help us to understand the four beasts in Daniel's night vision:

"**Babylon**" is symbolized by a *lion* with eagle's wings. The combination of a kingly beast and bird marks this kingdom with the same noble character as the **head of gold**. When the wings were plucked and the lion stood on its feet as a man, Babylon lost its lion's strength and the ability to rush and devour its prey like the eagle. A man's heart - weak and faint - replaced the lion's strength.

"**Media-Persia**" is symbolized by a *bear*, the same as the image's **silver chest and arms**. The bear "raised up on one side" indicates the double aspect of the Media-Persian Empire in which Persia rose higher to dominate the Medes. The three ribs in its mouth represent the kingdoms of Lydia, Babylonia and Egypt - which Media-Persia overcame in its rise to world dominion.

"**Greece**" is symbolized by a *leopard*, the same as the image's **thighs of brass**. Four wings of a fowl represent Alexander the Great's swiftness to conquer. The four heads depict the four [rulers in control] . . . of the empire after Alexander's death.

"**Rome**" is represented by a strong beast with "*great iron teeth.*" [The same as the image's **legs**.] Rome's destructiveness could not be compared with any animal. Its great iron teeth broke in pieces all the previous beasts, comments the *Search for Truth Home Bible Study.* (5)

The Word of God then informs us that added to this fourth

kingdom were ten horns and another little horn, which came up among them for a total of eleven horns. Speaking of the little horn, Daniel 7:8 states, " . . . in this horn were eyes like the eyes of man, and a mouth speaking great things [Antichrist]." It is common knowledge the ten horns (kings) = the feet (ten toes) of Nebuchadnezzar's image. Hence, Daniel 2:33 35; 7:23-27, and Rev. 17:12-14 teach that these powers are destroyed at the Second Coming of Christ.

Continuing to look at how Nebuchadnezzar's image mirrors Daniel's night visions, one should also note the order in which Daniel saw the four beasts. They *"form the image of the man"* in Nebuchadnezzar's dream, starting with his head and ending with the man's feet. (*Note the parenthesis):

Daniel's four night visions (Da. 7)	Nebuchadnezzar's image of a man (Da. 2)
1) The first beast **lion**, with one head.	Babylon **(head)**, with one ruler.
*Remember Daniel told **King** Nebuchadnezzar the **"ruler"** over Babylon, "Thou art this **"head"** of gold". So heads = rulers. (*Strong's Concordance* confirms this.)	
2) The second beast **bear**, with one head.	Medes and Persians **(arms and chest)**, with one ruler
3) The third beast **leopard**, with four heads.	Grecian Empire **(stomach and thighs)**, with four rulers/generals.
4) The fourth beast of *"great iron teeth,"* with one head. --and **ten horns** in his head (& the little horn came up among them).	Roman Empire **(legs)**, with one ruler. --Jews/Arabs **(feet)**.

It's time to study the fourth beast in a little bit more depth. Daniel 7:7-8 states,

> (v. 7) After this I saw in the night visions, and behold a fourth beast, dreadful and terrible, and strong exceedingly; and it had great **iron** teeth: it devoured and brake in

pieces, and stamped the residue with the feet of it: and it was diverse from all the beasts that were before it; **and it had ten horns**. (v. 8) I considered the horns, and, behold, there **came up among them another little horn**, before whom there were three of the first horns plucked up by the roots: and, behold, **in this horn were eyes like the eyes of man, and a mouth speaking great things**.

First of all, notice the fourth beast, symbolic for the former Roman Empire, was the *only one to retain its metal*; it was said to have had great *iron* teeth. Daniel 2:40 tells us all of the other kingdoms, Babylon, Media-Persia and Greece were broken or crushed. The Roman Empire, however, was *only bruised* because it still plays a major role in world government and religion today.

Secondly, Daniel 7:17 states, "These great beasts, which are four, are four kings." Daniel 7:23 tells us, " . . . [t]he fourth beast shall be the *fourth kingdom* upon earth." So here, beasts, kings, and kingdoms are *all* synonymous terms. *It is extremely important to understand that the ten horns included in the description of the fourth beast were not referred to as a fifth kingdom. This is because they were *in the head* of the fourth beast; hence Da. 7:20 states, "And of the ten horns that _WERE IN HIS HEAD_." In other words, the ten horns were under the _rule_ of the former Roman Empire.

The ten horns, being in the fourth beast's head, also indicated the fourth beast was "*keeping in memory*" this last day fifth and final evil kingdom!! Rev. 17:12 gives us more information: "And the ten horns which thou sawest are ten kings, which _have received no kingdom AS YET_; but receive power as kings one hour with the beast." Daniel 7:24 states, "And the ten horns out of this kingdom are ten kings that *shall* arise." The ten horns have to be in the fourth beast's head (*kingdom or memory*) until, in this last day, the Arabs and the Jews come together *to arise* and form their own kingdom. Satan is also "*keeping in memory*" his plan to possess the Israeli leader until he be taken out of the way (see II Thes. 2:7 on pg. 16, also the note on pg. 124).

So, when looking at Daniel's four beasts on pg. 118, what

we have are four kingdoms represented by *seven heads* (or seven rulers) "<u>and</u>" *ten horns* (plus one little horn). I would like to mention three other places in the Bible where we see the seven heads and ten horns arise:

<u>Revelation 12:3</u> - And there appeared another wonder in heaven, and behold a great red dragon, having seven heads and ten horns, and seven crowns upon his heads.

<u>Revelation 13:1</u> - And I stood upon the sand of the sea, and saw a beast rise up out of the sea, having seven heads and ten horns, and upon his horns ten crowns, and upon his heads the name of blasphemy.

<u>Revelation 17:3, 9, 10</u> – (v. 3) So he carried me away in the spirit into the wilderness: and I saw a *woman sit upon a scarlet coloured beast, full of names of **blasphemy**,* having seven heads and ten horns. (v. 9) And here is the mind which hath wisdom. The seven heads are seven mountains, on which the woman sitteth. (v. 10) And there are seven kings: five are fallen, and one is, and the other is not yet come; and when he cometh, he must continue a short space.

<u>IN THE FOLLOWING PAGES, PROOF WILL BE PROVIDED TO YOU THROUGH THE WORD OF GOD, THAT IN ALL THREE CASES, REVELATION CHAPTERS 12, 13 AND 17, GOD WAS REFERRING TO THE IMAGE IN NEBUCHADNEZZAR'S DREAM.</u>

To begin with, this beast has been around for a long time. Revelation chapter 12 tells us it was in heaven! In short, Revelation chapter 12:1-5 relates to us the woman (Israel) was to bring forth a man child, or Jesus Christ. The man child, "was to rule all nations with a rod of iron: and her child was caught up unto God, and to his throne" (Rev. 12:5). Prior to His being caught up, the great red dragon (Satan) stood before the woman to devour her child. Again, we turn to Revelation 12:3: " . . . behold a great red dragon, having **seven heads** and **ten horns** [the ten horns will be discussed later], and **seven crowns upon**

his heads." Notice, the **_seven heads_** had **_seven crowns_** representing the **_seven rulers_** of Daniel's image (refer to page 118).

*You may ask, "If, in Rev. 12:3, this is the exact same beast with seven heads, as in Revelation 17:9, then why aren't these seven crowned heads also denoted as the seven mountains that the woman, a city (Rev. 17:9, 18) sitteth upon?" And the answer is BECAUSE THE ROMAN CATHOLIC CHURCH WAS NOT IN EXISTENCE THEN! THE ROMAN CATHOLIC CHURCH WAS NOT AROUND AT THE TIME OF THE MAN-CHILD, JESUS CHRIST!

Rome is known as the city, which sits on <u>seven mountains</u>. She is referred to as **_"the city of the seven hills"_** (6). It is written in Daniel 2:43, the "seed of men"/the Roman Catholic Church, shall (*future*) mingle with the beast. Here in Rev. 12:3, the seven crowned heads are not considered seven mountains because at this time there was no Roman Catholic Church to mingle with the beast as in Rev. 17:3.

*<u>One must realize the seven heads, mentioned in Revelation chapters 12, 13 and 17, have a double meaning according to the time frame in which they appear.</u> The seven heads' double meaning becomes quite obvious when studying both Revelation 13 and 17. **In Revelation chapter 13, *the four beasts of Daniel chapter 7,* have united to become a single beast.** Revelation 13:1, 2 states,

> (v. 1) And I stood upon the sand of the sea, and saw *A BEAST* rise up out of the sea, having *seven heads* and *ten horns*, and upon his horns ten crowns, and upon his heads the name of "*blasphemy*" [man-made religion]. (v. 2) And the beast which I saw was like unto a *leopard*, and his feet were as the feet of a *bear*, and his mouth as the mouth of a *lion*: and the dragon gave him his power, and his seat, and great authority.

This verse specifically says there are "seven heads." Recall, Nebuchadnezzar, <u>ruler</u> over Babylon, was the <u>head</u> of gold. Therefore, the seven heads equal the seven rulers of Nebuchadnezzar's image: **a)** Babylon/lion = <u>one</u> head (or ruler);

121

b) Medes and Persians/bear = <u>one</u> head; **c)** Grecian Empire/leopard = <u>four</u> heads, for a total of only ***SIX HEADS***. .... Where is the seventh head? .... IT'S CARRYING THE WOMAN!! The great iron teeth, specifically the Western Roman Empire, containing the seventh head or seven mountains is carrying the Roman Catholic Church. Hence, *upon his heads the name of blasphemy* (Rev. 13:1). The woman, a city, sits upon seven mountains, full of the names of blasphemy (Rev. 17:3, 9, 18).

Furthermore, in Rev. 13:2, only three beasts are apparent: the leopard, bear and lion. <u>Daniel's fourth beast</u>, the great iron teeth of Daniel ch. 7, is missing again because the former Roman Empire is carrying the Mother of Harlots. ***The seven heads mentioned in Revelation 13:1, 2 have a "double meaning":***

--First of all, the <u>seven heads</u> are symbolic of the *<u>seven mountains</u>* of Rome on which the woman (blasphemy) sitteth.

--Second of all, the seven heads are symbolic of the *<u>seven rulers</u>* concealed in Daniel's four beasts. The fourth beast, the great iron teeth, had *one head* or ruler, which was missing from the equation.

    d) former Roman Empire/great iron teeth = 1 head; (for a total now of seven heads).

Now notice, on pg. 120, the heads in Revelation 13:1 are not referred to as kings as in Rev. 12:3, nor as mountains as in Rev. 17:9; this is because the heads are now symbolic of both! Revelation chapter 17 confirms the double meaning of the heads. Revelation 17:3 says, " . . . and I saw a woman 'sit upon' [or ***CARRIED*** by (Rev. 17:7)] a scarlet coloured beast, full of names of BLASPHEMY, having **seven heads** and ten horns." Pay attention to the double meaning in Revelation 17:9, 10:

(v. 9) And here is the mind which hath wisdom. The seven heads are ***<u>seven mountains</u>***, on which the woman sitteth [Western Roman Empire]. (v. 10) **And** [OR PLUS] there are ***<u>seven kings</u>***: **five are fallen** [Medes/Persians = 1 i.e. ruler; Grecian Empire = 4; total = 5], **and one is** [Roman Empire = 1 ruler; Daniel 2:40 he was only *bruised*], **and the other is not yet come** ["Mystery" Babylon =

Antichrist = 1 ruler as the *head*]; and when **he** cometh, he must continue a short space.

So, not only are the "seven heads" symbolic of the seven mountains/hills of Rome, but also the seven heads are symbolic of the seven rulers/kings of Nebuchadnezzar's image. The representation of the heads as mountains, rulers, or both depends entirely upon the time in which they arise.

To conclude the discussion of how Nebuchadnezzar's image travels through time, focus your attention on the "**ten horns**" or feet of the man. Pay particular attention to the time frame of their crowning. Revelation 17:12, 13 states, "(v. 12) And the ten horns which thou sawest are ten kings, which have received *no kingdom as yet*; BUT RECEIVE POWER AS KINGS ONE HOUR WITH THE BEAST. (v. 13) These have one mind, and shall give their power and strength unto the beast." When Benjamin Netanyahu moves into position heading up the beast, the ten horns shall finally receive their crowns and their kingdom.

Revelation chapter 13:1, 2 houses the evidence:

(v. 1) And I stood upon the sand of the sea, and saw "**A BEAST**" [they all came together in unity] rise up out of the sea, having *seven heads* and *ten horns*, and *UPON HIS HORNS TEN CROWNS* [they received their kingdom], and upon his heads the name of *blasphemy*. (v. 2) And the beast which I saw was like unto a *leopard*, and his feet were as the feet of a *bear*, and HIS MOUTH AS THE MOUTH OF A *LION* [because he has "a mouth speaking great things", see Daniel 7:8]: and the dragon gave him his power, and his seat, and great authority."

Recall the previous study identified *all of the seven heads* mentioned in the above verse (note italicized/underlined words). This same verse also displays the ten horns with crowns, having their kingdom. Yet, what about the little horn?? *Where is the little horn from which they received their kingdom? Where is the little horn, the Antichrist, which completes Daniel's night vision (Da. 7:7, 8) of the four beasts? He is not outwardly mentioned in these verses. The reason why you cannot find the *little horn* is because he is hiding in the *head* of the LION!!

Benjamin Netanyahu is in the head of the lion! Da. 7:8 and Rev. 13:2 declares that *the little horn has a "mouth" speaking great things*; his mouth will be as the mouth of a lion.

In taking Daniel's place as the third ruler over "<u>Babylon</u>", Benjamin Netanyahu will be of the **seven heads** because he will be the "<u>head of gold</u>" (the lion). However, he will be of the **eighth** because when he arises and takes his position to "speak great things," he will be the eighth ruler to this final man-made kingdom. Revelation 17:10 states, "And there are seven kings [or rulers, see Nebuchadnezzar's image page 126]: five are fallen, and one is, and the other is not yet come [Antichrist/heading up Mystery Babylon]; and when **"he"** cometh, he must continue a short space." And verse 11 tells us,

> And the beast that *was* [because from **"head"** to feet, this image was in heaven (see Revelation 12)], and *is not* [because throughout time the beast used different people to accomplish certain tasks], even *he* [Benjamin Netanyahu, replacing Daniel the prophet as **head**, or ruler, of Mystery Babylon] is the *eighth* [king, because kings were the topic in verse 10], and is of the *seven* [because "he", Benjamin Netanyahu taking the prophet Daniel's place, is the head of gold], and goeth into perdition.

<u>Note</u>: Benjamin Netanyahu will move into position shortly after Satan is cast out of heaven to this earth. Rev. 12:12 says the devil will come *down* unto us having great wrath, and he can only continue a *short time*. This is the same event in Rev. 17:10. When Netanyahu moves into position, he can only exist for a *short space*. Unlike his followers in Rev. 17:7, 8, who will ascend from the bottomless pit, the Antichrist, in Satan's memory, is not yet come (Rev. 17:10). Rev. 17:10, 11 continues in sequence showing that when he gets here, *he is of the seven kings*; yet he is the eighth.

<u>Special note</u>: Some may say the woman in Rev. 17:3 is Israel. YET, HOW CAN ISRAEL *CARRY* ISRAEL? The feet made of Arabs and *Jews* will *carry* the woman, or the Roman Catholic Church. Rev. 17:7 states, "I will tell thee the mystery of the woman, and of the beast that *carrieth* [meaning foot (7) (the feet carry)] her, which hath the seven

124

heads and ten horns." Rev. 17:12, "And the ten horns which thou sawest are ***ten kings*** [meaning foot (8)] . . . . " The feet made of ***Jews*** will ***carry*** the woman, the Roman Catholic Church. Thus, the woman cannot possibly be Israel, for how can Israel *carry* Israel. They cannot carry themselves.

THE BEAST WITHIN THE MAN

Nebuchadnezzar = Yitzhak Rabin
Belshazzar = Shimon Peres
Daniel/prophet = Benjamin Netanyahu

Nebuchadnezzar's Dream	Daniel's Four Visions (Rev. 17:10, 11 (7 kings)	
GOLD (Babylon = 1 ruler)	LION (1 head) *Heads are symbolic for rulers!	". . . the other is not yet come; & when "he" cometh, . . . he is the 8th [king], & is of the 7, [because he (little horn) is the head of gold (LION)]."
SILVER (Media-Persia = 1 ruler)	BEAR (1 head)	"5 have fallen"
BRASS (Greece = 4 rulers)	LEOPARD (4 heads)	
IRON (Roman Empire = one ruler)	IRON TEETH "1 is" (1 head) The 10 (horns/kings) are in his head; **for, they have no kingdom as yet**, see (Rev. 17:12, 13).	
FEET Part of Iron ///////////// & Part of Clay ///////////// *shall* mingle with seed of men (E. Roman Empire) (Jews) (Roman Cath. Church)		

1.) Nebuchadnezzar **imagined** his own kingdom. He touched God's vessels of service placing them in the house of his god.	1.) Rabin imagined a different kingdom. He touched the land, which was set aside for God's service.
2.) Belshazzar, worse than his predecessor, touched & drank from God's vessels. In Da. 5:28, Belshazzar was associated with the word "*Peres.*" His ungodly act caused the land to be divided among the enemy.	2.) "Peres" saw Rabin's death. Still he, worse than Rabin, was a "raiser of taxes". He was the *driving* force behind the New Middle East. In fulfillment of prophecy, Peres divided the land amongst the enemy.
3.) Daniel, a Jew, was made the third ruler over the Babylonian kingdom. Even so, he never took the position.	3.)Benjamin Netanyahu, a Jew, is the third ruler of this man-made kingdom, Mystery Babylon.

*Rev. 17:10, 11, "(v. 10) And there are **seven kings**: five are fallen [Medes / Persia / Grecian], and one is [Rome], and the other is not yet come [Mystery Babylon]; and when he cometh, he must continue a short space. (v. 11) And the beast that was, and is not, even he is the eighth **[king]**, and is of the seven [Babylon "head" of gold], and goeth into perdition.

Chapter 11
The Beginning of the End

Daniel 9:27 reads, "And he [the Antichrist] shall confirm [strengthen (1)] the covenant [treaty (2)] with *__many__* for one week: and in the midst of the week he shall cause the sacrifice and the oblation to cease . . . ."

When Benjamin Netanyahu agreed to the pre-existing treaty that surrendered Hebron, I believe it was then he confirmed the "covenant" of Daniel 9:27. There is a great deal of evidence his approval of this already-existing *treaty* that gave the Israelis' **birthright** or land to the Palestinians triggered the final seven year period prior to Christ's return. The usability of the following material will help to establish this statement.

First of all, the word *__many__* used in the above verse will help us identify more readily the "treaty" referred to in Daniel 9:27. In the Hebrew, the word *many* means *prince* (3). As expressed earlier, Shimon Peres is the ***prince*** of the covenant of the peace treaty signing between the Arabs and the Jews. It has been written:

> . . . "many" comes from "rabim," and the Hebrew word root . . . "rab," meaning "great" . . . . It also indicates men of great wisdom and leadership potential. From this root, comes the modern word "rabbi." [I]srael's [former] Prime Minister, Yitzhak Rabin, has a surname that originates from this same word root. And it is . . . one of the important signatures on the Covenant. Jewish commentaries translate "rabim," ("the great ones") as the leaders of Israel . . . . **He [the Antichrist] will agree with [the prince and] the "rabim," or highest leaders of Israel, assuring them that he will honor their covenant**. (4)

Secondly and most importantly, after studying the following stories, *__which have the same theme interwoven throughout__*, I realized Benjamin Netanyahu was on a planned course, headed straight for destruction. I have titled this reoccurring theme,

"THE DOUBLE BETRAYAL."

When Benjamin Netanyahu agreed to the preexisting treaty, concerning the pull out of Hebron, I felt certain that this was *the beginning of the end*. Netanyahu's agreeing to give away the *Israeli birthright* was certainly a betrayal. However, in looking at Daniel ch. 11, I could not account for his confirmation of the peace treaty as the beginning of the final seven-year period. Only one betrayal became truly obvious in this chapter and that was more of a spiritual betrayal, not one concerning the land. This spiritual betrayal occurs in Daniel chapter 11:27, 28. This is where the Prime Minister of Israel sits at a table with the king of the south and betrays the "cause" which is God reuniting mankind to Himself (see Da. 11:27, 28, pgs. 41-45).

Then I realized there will be a double betrayal, first with the birthright and then with the blessing. The Israeli birthright, Hebron, surrendered to the opposition appears to have marked the first betrayal. (Still, there is the Wye River Accord to consider which he signed on October 23, 1998. This accord transferred to the Palestinians broad areas of the land of Israel.) Nevertheless, looking at the betrayal of surrendering Hebron, the Promised Land, to the opposition was I believe identified only in a different chapter of the Bible other than Da. Chapter 11. Keep in mind however, the blessing, or betraying of the "cause," again occurs in Da. 11:27, 28, and this is the *second* betrayal.

The following allegories establish there will be a double betrayal. Examine Judas' life. He had betrayed Christ times two. He betrayed our Lord first when he went to the chief priest and then again sitting at the table with Jesus. This same theme occurs with Jacob! Esau stated in Genesis 27:36, ". . . Is not he rightly named Jacob? for he hath supplanted me these **TWO TIMES**: he took away my **BIRTHRIGHT**; and, behold, now he hath taken away my **BLESSING**." Looking at the three stories of Esau/Jacob, and of Judas, and of the Antichrist, a double betrayal became very apparent, **first** with the birthright, **then** with the blessing.

Brother Mendenhall, a pastor from a United Pentecostal Church, helps to display the birthright as a separate entity from the blessing with the following message:

128

Jacob wanted the blessings of Isaac upon him. He connived and acted as Esau. He *already had* the birthright, but now he wanted the blessing. Esau never [really] complained about losing his birthright because the blessing would be more important than his birthright. When he got angry, it was not because he lost so many acres of land and so much sheep and so much oxen, that wasn't a big deal with him. But he became very, very angry because he lost the blessing of Isaac upon him. [In] Genesis 49, Jacob got old, called in 12 sons to bless them and not to divide up inheritance that was already taken care of. The law of customs had already taken care of that. [In] Genesis chapter 49, we read [about] the <u>blessing, which is much more important than his finances</u>. Genesis 49:28, when Jacob called his sons into bless them: all of these are the 12 tribes of Israel and this is it that their father Jacob spake unto them and blessed them everyone according to **his blessing = he blessed them**. He did not divide up his estate; that was not what he was doing. He was giving them a spiritual blessing and that spiritual blessing was then to be passed on to his 12 sons and he blessed them with the blessing that he had been blessed by. (5)

Even though the spiritual blessing followed and was closely connected to the birthright, they were not the same things. Realizing this will help us to understand the path that Benjamin Netanyahu will take. Study the next page carefully.

THE DOUBLE BETRAYAL

1) The Birthright (such things as: land, money, oxen, etc.)
2) Spiritual Blessing
3) The stories of Esau/Jacob and of Judas work together in bringing enlightenment to prophesies concerning the Antichrist!

First Betrayal - The Birthright
(a+b=c)

a) Esau (Arabs/Yasser Arafat) and Jacob (Jews/Benjamin Netanyahu) made a deal and the *firstborn* sold or "*surrendered*" his *birthright* (inherited land).

b) Judas made a *covenant* with the opposition. He betrayed and set up the <u>Lamb</u> of God for the slaughter. Thereby, he surrendered his birthright of a future earthly kingdom restored to Israel. "[O]T prophets predicted a future kingdom which God would set up on earth (Isa. 9:6-8; Dan. 2:44)" (6). (See the kingdom of God on page 132.)

c) Benjamin Netanyahu, the "*firstborn*," agreed to an already existing peace treaty (or covenant) between the Arabs and the Jews. He *surrendered* the inherited land, i.e., spec. Hebron, the Jewish birthright. With his first betrayal, he set up God's <u>sheep</u> for the slaughter! (*Recall Zech. 11 on pgs. 58-63*).

Second Betrayal and even more significant - The Spiritual Blessing
(a+b=c)

a) Isaac was preparing for his unknown day of death. He wanted to bless his firstborn son with the blessings promised by God to his father, Abraham. The most important was the spiritual blessing. The "anointed one" or *chief ruler (I Chron. 5:1-2)* would come through the family line. Jacob desiring to be supreme, wore Esau's garments and brought goats meat to deceive his father into blessing him. Profaning God's name, he claimed, "the LORD thy God **BROUGHT** (the meat/temple)." Calling himself the "**I AM**," he kissed his father with the kiss of death.

b) Sitting at a table, with his heart being now evil, Judas lied to Jesus Christ as he partook of the sop. Judas just didn't betray Christ, the "anointed one," **he betrayed the *cause***, or God reuniting man back unto Himself. For riches, 30 pieces of silver, the Lamb was slain. It was the kiss of death, and Jesus Christ the Temple (John 2:19), was desecrated.

c) Benjamin Netanyahu, who holds the bag, will sit at a table; his heart shall be to do mischief. Speaking lies, he shall sell out the *cause*, God bringing man back to Himself. But, it shall not prosper. For riches, "his heart shall be against the holy covenant." To Israel, he will profane God's name and claim "the LORD thy God "**BROUGHT**" the temple." Netanyahu, in wanting to be supreme, will call himself the "I AM." Israel, desiring to bless their firstborn son, will acknowledge him as their King and High Priest. Thus, their unknown day of death will then be upon them.

What Is the Kingdom of God?

In the days of Christ, the Jewish people were under Roman rule, and they wanted out from under it. The disciples inquired of the Lord in Acts 1.6, 7, "[L]ord, wilt thou at this time restore again the kingdom to Israel? And he said unto them, It is not for you to know the times or the seasons, which the Father hath put in his own power." Then in Luke 11:20 and 17:21, God informs us the kingdom of God is power, and it is within the saints of God.

Together, Luke 11 and Rev. 12 reveal a day in the future when the kingdom of God *shall* also come upon us.

Luke 11:20 states:

> But if I with the finger of *God CAST OUT DEVILS*, no doubt the *kingdom of God is come upon you*.

Rev. 12:7-10 states:

> (v. 7) And there was war in heaven: Michael and his angels fought against the dragon; and the dragon fought and his angels, (v. 8) And prevailed not; neither was their place found any more in heaven. (v. 9) And the great dragon was *CAST OUT*, that old serpent, called the *DEVIL,* and Satan, which deceiveth the whole world: he was cast out into the earth, and his angels were cast out with him. (v. 10) And I heard a loud voice saying in heaven, *NOW is come* salvation, and strength, and the *kingdom of our God*, and the power of his Christ: for the accuser of our brethren is cast down, which accused them before our God day and night.

One day the *devil* and his angels will be permanently *cast out* of heaven. When this event transpires, the Word of God says "NOW" is come the kingdom of our God. A greater manifestation of the kingdom of God will occur at this time. For, the kingdom of God is like a mustard seed; it starts off small and then *increases with time*.

Mark 4:26-32 states:

> (v. 26) And he said, So is the kingdom of God, as if a man

132

should cast seed into the ground; (v. 27) And should sleep, and rise night and day, and the seed should spring and grow up, he knoweth not how. (v. 28) For the earth bringeth forth fruit of herself; first the blade, then the ear, after that the full corn in the ear. (v. 29) But when the fruit is brought forth, immediately he putteth in the sickle, because the harvest is come. (v. 30) And he said, Whereunto shall we liken the kingdom of God? or with what comparison shall we compare it? (v. 31) It is like a grain of mustard seed, which, when it is sown in the earth, is less than all the seeds that be in the earth: (v. 32) But when it is sown, it groweth up, and becometh greater than all herbs, and shooteth out great branches; so that the fowls of the air may lodge under the shadow of it.

We see the kingdom of God's continual growth <u>with time</u> in the words that Jesus spoke to Pilate, the Roman governor. Jesus stated, "My kingdom is not of *this world*; if my kingdom were of *this world*, then would my servants fight, that I should not be delivered to the Jews: but *"NOW"* is my kingdom not from hence" (John 18:36). Jesus was saying at that present time, when He walked the earth, the kingdom of God was *not* of **THIS WORLD**. Yet, Rev. 11:15 tells us there is a day coming when "[t]he kingdoms of *this world* are become the kingdoms of our Lord . . . and he shall reign for ever and ever." So the kingdom of God is truly like a mustard seed. It increases with time:

-The kingdom of God is within us.
-When the devil is cast out, it shall come upon us.
-In that day, the kingdoms of "this world" shall become the kingdoms of our Lord.

Daniel chapter 2:44 testifies of a *future earthly* kingdom: "And in the days of *these kings shall* the God of heaven <u>*set up a kingdom*</u> . . . [and] it shall break in pieces and consume all these kingdoms, and it shall stand for ever." As was stated in Chapter 10, God is going to set up a future earthly kingdom at a time when Nebuchadnezzar's image is in power. Referring to just the ten kings in the feet of Nebuchadnezzar's image, Rev. 12 tells us that these ten kings do not have a kingdom yet. However, they will receive their crowns and power when the Antichrist moves into his position, the "head" of authority in the image. At the end of the beasts' three and one half year reign, God will then return to destroy their kingdom and establish His own. Thus, this proves there is a future earthly kingdom waiting to be restored.

Lord wilt thou at this time restore again the kingdom to Israel? The time shall surely come when God's people will no longer be under "Roman rule" or the *law of this land*, but we shall be under the rule of our Lord.

Chapter 12
One Way in the Temple, One Way Out

Ephesians 4:4-5, There is one body, and one Spirit, even as ye are called in one hope of your calling; One Lord, one faith, one baptism.

One Spirit

The Bible establishes that God is not a person; He is Spirit which is present everywhere. David stated in Psalm 139:7, 8, "(v. 7) Whither shall I go from thy spirit? or whither shall I flee from thy presence? (v. 8) If I ascend up into heaven, thou art there: if I make my bed in hell, behold, thou art there." Proverbs 15:3 reads, "The eyes of the LORD are in every place." I Kings 8:27 states, "But will God indeed dwell on the earth? behold, the heaven and heaven of heavens cannot contain thee; how much less this house that I have builded?" John 4:24 states, "**God is a spirit.**" I Corinthians 12:13 emphasizes, "For by **one Spirit** are we all baptized into one body, whether we be Jews or Gentiles, whether we be bond or free; and have been all made to drink into one Spirit." II Corinthians 3:17 states, "Now the Lord is that Spirit: and where the Spirit of the Lord is, there is liberty."

One Lord

In comparing the LORD Jehovah of the Old Testament to the Lord Jesus of the New Testament, we will establish there is only one Lord. Isaiah 12:2, "the LORD JEHOVAH . . . he also is become my salvation." Thus, Jesus is Lord!

1) **Old Testament**: Deuteronomy 4:39 states, "Know therefore this day, and consider it in thine heart, that the LORD he is God in heaven above, and upon the earth beneath: *there is none else.*"

   New Testament: In John 20:28, Thomas knew who Jesus was when he said unto Him, ". . . My Lord and my God."

2) **Old Testament**: Deuteronomy 6:4 reminds us, "Hear, O Israel: The LORD our God is one LORD."

   New Testament: Because of the first commandment's significance and unchanging nature, Jesus reiterates this in the New Testament (see Mark 12:29-37). Philippians 2:11 states it best: "[J]esus Christ is Lord."

3) **Old Testament**: Deuteronomy 32:39 states, "See now that I, even I, am he, and there is no god with me: I kill, and I make alive; I wound, and I heal."

   New Testament: Luke 7:21, "And in that same hour he cured many of their infirmities."

4) **Old Testament**: Isaiah 43:10 states, "Ye are my witnesses, saith the LORD, and my servant whom I have chosen; that ye may know and believe me, and understand <u>that I am he: before me there was no God formed, neither shall there be *after* me</u>."

   New Testament: John 8:24, 27 states, "I said therefore unto you, that ye shall die in your sins: for if ye believe not that <u>I am he</u>, ye shall die in your sins. They understood not that he spake to them of <u>the Father</u>."

5) **Old Testament**: Isaiah 45:18 states, "For thus saith the LORD that created the heavens; God himself that formed the earth and made it."

    New Testament: Colossians 1:16 speaks of Jesus: "For by him were all things created, that are in heaven, and that are in earth."

6) **Old Testament**: Isaiah 44:6, "Thus saith the LORD the King of Israel, and his redeemer the LORD of hosts; I am the first, and I am the last; and beside me there is no God."

    New Testament: Jesus stated in Revelation 1:11, "I am Alpha and Omega, the first and the last." And He was also called the King, in I Timothy 6:14-16.

7) **Old Testament**: Isaiah 43:11, "I, even I, am the LORD; *and beside me there is no saviour.*"

    New Testament: Philippians 3:20 states, "For our conversation is in heaven; from whence also we look for *the Savior*, the Lord Jesus Christ."

8) **Old Testament**: Isaiah 44:24 states, "Thus saith the LORD, thy Redeemer, and he that formed thee from the womb." Isaiah 12:2 says, "Behold, God is my salvation; I will trust, and not be afraid: for the LORD JEHOVAH is my strength and my song; he also is become my salvation."

    New Testament: *The Revell Bible Dictionary* reports, "[J]esus, from the Hebrew word yeshua', meaning 'savior' or 'Yahweh [the LORD; Jehovah] saves' . . ." (1). Jesus saves (see Luke 19:10), and He forgave sins (see Luke 5:20; 7:48).

One Faith

The apostle writes in Matthew 16:15-18:

> (v. 15) He saith unto them, But whom say ye that I am? (v. 16) And Simon Peter answered and said, Thou art the Christ, the Son of the living God. (v. 17) And Jesus answered and said unto him, Blessed art thou, Simon Barjona: for flesh and blood hath not *revealed* it unto thee, but my Father which is in heaven. (v. 18) And I say also unto thee, That thou art Peter, and upon this rock [*Peter's revelation*] I will build my church."

Peter understood Jesus was the Christ. If you are going to be part of the church, you must also have faith that Jesus is the Christ, or *anointed one*, the Son of the Living God. The disciples referred to Him as the Christ because they knew He was the promised Messiah of the Old Testament. According to Old Testament prophesies, the Messiah (or anointed one in Hebrew) would come to deliver the people and reclaim the *throne* of David (Ps. 2:2-6; *Christ the King*, Isa. 9:7; Isa. 61:1).

When Jesus Christ came to the earth, John the Baptist had faith that Jesus was the deliverer. John, upon seeing Jesus, said boldly, "Behold the Lamb of God, which taketh away the sin of the world" (John 1:29). Andrew, a follower of Jesus, stated, "We have found the Messias, which is, being interpreted, the Christ" (John 1:41). When one acknowledges Jesus as the Christ, or the anointed one of the Old Testament, this is a statement of faith in believing that Jesus has a divine nature with the power to save. And if we look at Jesus as Savior, then He must be Jehovah in the flesh, because only the LORD of the Old Testament had the power to save (pg. 137, #'s 7, 8). Only God could forgive sins, and the Pharisees knew this. That is why they challenged Jesus' divinity when Christ stated, " . . . Man, thy sins are forgiven thee" (Luke 5:20). In verse 21 the scribes and Pharisees asked in an uproar, "Who is this which speaketh blasphemies? Who can forgive sins, but God alone?"

John 1:10 states, "He was in the world, and the world was made by him, and the world knew him not." Jesus Christ was

God in the flesh. You see the quality of God was in Christ and not the quantity because God is an invisible, immortal Spirit, which fills all space. You cannot put all of God in a box, house, or anything else because He is everywhere at all times. II Corinthians 5:19 states, "God was in Christ, reconciling the world unto himself." John 1:1, 14 shows the incarnation of God: "(v. 1) In the beginning was the Word [or thought; plan (2)], and the Word was with God, and the Word was God. (v. 14) And the Word was made flesh, and dwelt among us." God is a spirit. The Word was His thoughts, and His thoughts were expressed in the man Christ Jesus. Understand God was 100% man; He cried, slept, ate and prayed. The Bible says that man should pray without ceasing. Christ's humanity was praying to deity to gain strength, support and guidance. However, as God, because divinity dwelt inside of humanity, He created all things, wrought miracles and had the power to redeem the lost. Jesus stated, " . . . for if ye believe not that I am he, ye shall die in your sins . . . . They understood not that he spake to them of the Father" (John 8:24, 27).

We must have the faith that Christ is able to save us. If we have that faith, then we need to act upon it. James 2:19 states, "Thou believest that there is one God; thou doest well: the devils also believe, and tremble." The devils believe there is only one God. Obviously the devil is not saved. James 2:20 states, "faith without works is dead." Faith must have an action. We will see what that action is in the next section.

One Baptism

Acts 2:38, 39 states,

> Then Peter [who had the keys to the kingdom of heaven] said unto them, Repent, and be baptized every one of you in the name of Jesus Christ for the remission of sins, and ye shall receive the gift of the Holy Ghost. For the promise is unto you, and to your children, and to all that are afar off, even as many as the Lord our God shall call.

On the day of Pentecost, Peter was preaching to them the plan of salvation. Spoken in his words, we find the gospel. Peter was telling them to identify with and obey the ***GOSPEL***.

Notice:

1) The <u>repentance</u> identifies with Christ's **death**. We need to confess to the Lord that we are sinners. Romans 7:15-20 tells us that there is no good thing which dwelleth in man. Knowing this, we need to ask Jesus Christ to be our Savior and the Lord of our life. We must die out to our own will and live according to His.

2) The <u>baptism</u> identifies with His **burial**. We need to be "fully immersed" in water, and take on His name in baptism (Acts 2:38). Romans 6:4 states, "Therefore we are "buried" with him by baptism." (Just as in the natural, no one was ever buried by having a little dirt sprinkled on him or her.)

3) The <u>in filling of the Holy Ghost</u> is our partaking of the **resurrection**. Romans 8:11 says that if the same Spirit is in us that was in Christ, so shall we like Him rise from the dead.

Paul declared this gospel of the death, burial and resurrection in I Corinthians 15:1-4:

(v. 1) Moreover, brethren, I *declare unto you the gospel* which I preached unto you, which also ye have received, and wherein ye stand; (v. 2) By which also ye are saved, if ye keep in memory what I preached unto you, unless ye have BELIEVED in vain. (v. 3) For I delivered unto you first of all that which I also received, how that Christ DIED for our sins according to the scriptures; (v. 4) And that he was BURIED, and that he ROSE AGAIN.

II Thessalonians 1:7, 8 warns us God is coming back: " . . . taking vengeance on them that know not God, and that **obey** not the gospel of our Lord Jesus Christ." We OBEY the gospel by doing what Peter said in Acts 2:38, 39.

On the day of Pentecost, Peter was fulfilling the command that Jesus had spoken: "Go ye therefore, and teach all nations, baptizing them in the **NAME** of the Father, and of the Son, and of the Holy Ghost" (Matthew 28:19). Notice the word <u>name</u> is singular. If I was to go to the house of a man by the name of Mike, who was married with kids, and I asked his children, "What is the **name** *of* your *father*?" The children would reply, "Mike." If I were to go to the man's mother and say, "What is the **name** *of* your *son*?" She would say, "Mike." If I were to go to his wife and say, "What is the **name** *of* your *husband*?" She would say, "Mike." You see Jesus wanted them to use His "*name*" in baptism. Jesus is the name of the Father, and of the Son, and of the Holy Ghost. *John 5:43, Matthew 1:21 and John 14:26 declare this:

    -John 5:43, "I am come in my Father's name."
    -Matthew 1:21, "And she shall bring forth a son, and thou shalt call his name JESUS."
    -John 14:26, "But the Comforter, which is the Holy Ghost, whom the Father will send *in my name*."

Acts 4:12 states, "there is none other name under heaven given among men, whereby we must be saved." From the time of our Lord's death, we will never find in the entire Bible, anyone baptized in the titles Father, Son and Holy Ghost or any other way. They were only baptized in the *name of* Jesus Christ (see Luke 24:47; Acts 2:38; 8:12-17; 10:43-48; 19:2-6; 22:16).

Not only must we repent and be baptized in the name of Jesus Christ, but we must also receive the Holy Ghost. Romans 8:9 makes this clear: "Now if any man have not the Spirit of Christ, he is none of his." Christ said in John 3:5, 8, "Except a man be born of water and of the Spirit, he cannot enter into the kingdom of God. The wind bloweth where it listeth, and thou hearest the *sound* thereof, but canst not tell whence it cometh, and whither it goeth: so is every one that is born of the Spirit." Jesus said when you are born of the Spirit, there will be a *sound*. He tells us what that sound is in John 7:38, 39: "He that believeth on me, as the scripture hath said, out of his belly shall flow rivers of living water. (But this spake he of the Spirit, which they that believe on him should receive: for the Holy Ghost was not yet given; because that Jesus was not yet glorified.)" When one believes on Jesus according to the scriptures, then he shall receive the Holy Ghost. It is the Spirit of God that will flow up out of his belly, and when this happens to him a sound will be heard.

John the Baptist spoke unto the people: "I indeed baptize you with water unto repentance: but he that cometh after me is mightier than I, whose shoes I am not worthy to bear: he shall baptize you with the Holy Ghost, and with *fire*" (Matthew 3:11) On the day of Pentecost, "there came a sound from heaven as of a rushing mighty wind, and it filled all the house where they were sitting. And there appeared unto them *cloven tongues like as of fire*, and it sat upon each of them. And they were all filled with the Holy Ghost, and began to speak with other tongues" (Acts 2:2-4). In Acts 10:44-46, Peter went to Cornelius' house, a Gentile. While Peter yet spoke the Word to Cornelius and his family, the Holy Ghost fell on them that heard the Word. The disciples then realized the Gentiles had received the Holy Ghost, "For they *heard* them speak with tongues" (Acts 10:46). Isaiah 28:11-12 testifies of this day, "(v. 11) For with stammering lips and another tongue will he speak to this people. (v. 12) To whom he said, This is the rest wherewith ye may cause the weary to rest; and this is the refreshing: yet they would not hear" (see also Mark 16:17; John 14:16-18; 14:26; Acts 19:6). Let no man deceive you; prophecies, tongues and knowledge shall not cease until "that which is perfect is come [Jesus Christ]" (I Cor. 13:8-10).

> Jesus said, " . . . ye shall know the truth, and the truth shall make you free" (John 8:32). If you have not repented, been baptized in Jesus' name and filled with the Holy Ghost, then you need to contact your local Apostolic Pentecostal or United Pentecostal Church!

A Word to the Wise

The Word of God says that an individual will not be able to buy or sell except he or she takes the mark of the beast. If the individual takes the mark of the beast, the same shall drink of the wine of the wrath of God (Rev. 13:16, 17; Rev. 14:10). Therefore, I strongly suggest to the reader of this book to start stocking food and water in preparation for that spoken of day. Throughout the Word of God, humanity and deity has worked together. One given example is found in I Kings chapter 17. Elijah who stood upon the Word of God said there would be neither "dew nor rain" throughout the land. Because of the drought, famine then occurred and God sent Elijah to a widow woman's home. Elijah told the widow to make him a cake using her last morsel of bread along with the little oil that she owned. Now this woman was desperate because this was all that she and her son had to eat. I Kings 17:13-15 states:

> (v. 13) And Elijah said unto her, Fear not; go and do as thou hast said: but make me thereof a little cake first, and bring it unto me, and after make for thee and for thy son.
> (v. 14) For thus saith the LORD God of Israel, The barrel of meal shall not waste, neither shall the cruse of oil fail, until the day that the LORD sendeth rain upon the earth.
> (v. 15) And she went and did according to the saying of Elijah: and she, and he, and her house, did eat many days.

Elijah wanted the woman to *utilize all* that she had, according to the will of the Lord. When she, through faith, *obeyed* God's spoken Word, God then intervened on her behalf to bless her and her family. Another example of God's faithfulness, through mankind's obedience is found in Gen. ch. 41. According to the will of the Lord, Joseph instructed humanity to store food in preparation of the famine that was to come. God's blessing was seen only after the people through faith harkened unto God's Word. Again, humanity and deity worked together.

Will you help convert a lost soul over to the Lord?

For the first time ever, the Lord is unveiling these mysteries in preparation for battle. God has chosen you, this generation, to bring forth His endtime message. Our mission at ENDTIME CRUSADERS is to regain what Satan has stolen. Our desire is to see mankind reunited to God in these last and final days. We are looking for a mighty harvest, and we need your help to spread God's endtime message. James 5:20 states, "Let him know, that he which converteth the sinner from the error of his way shall save a soul from death, and shall hide a multitude of sins." If you would like to join in the battle for saving lost souls, please do the following, and I know the Lord will bless you greatly for it.

1) Find a prayer partner and pray for this ministry along with its purpose.
2) Send a one time, weekly or monthly donation to ENDTIME CRUSADERS, Inc., P.O. Box 1035, Safety Harbor, FL 34695.

Endtime Crusaders appreciates your support, and are looking forward to hearing from you!

A COPY OF THE OFFICIAL REGISTRATION AND FINANCIAL INFORMATION MAY BE OBTAINED FROM THE DIVISION OF CONSUMER SERVICES BY CALLING TOLL-FREE WITHIN THE STATE. REGISTRATION DOES NOT IMPLY ENDORSEMENT, APPROVAL, OR RECOMMENDATION BY THE STATE. 1-800-435-7352.

Endnotes

Note: All scripture is taken from the Thompson Chain-Reference Bible King James Version unless otherwise noted. Also for this section of endnotes, I give the full reference the first time a book is used. The endnote comes after the defining of the word.

Chapter 1

1) Twentier, Jerry, and Willhoite, Marcella. *Search for Truth*, 1985, 247.

2) *Strong's Exhaustive Concordance of the Bible*, pg. 1078, Greek Section pg. 71, #5016.

3) *Strong's Exhaustive Concordance*, pg. 959, Greek Section pg. 79, #5604.

4) Hagee, John, *Beginning of the End [-] The Assassination of Yitzhak Rabin and the Coming Antichrist*, Thomas Nelson Publishers, 1996, 97.

5) An Associated Press, "Clinton pledges flood aid," *The Tampa Tribune-Times*, April 23, 1997, 2.

6) *Weekly Compilation of Presidential Documents*, Monday, April 28, 1997, Volume 33, Number 17, 567-568.

7) Associated Press, "On balance, the planet is in trouble, group's report says," *St. Petersburg Times*, May 19, 1996, Section 4A.

8) Collie, Tim, "2nd storm finishes devastation of N.C. farming region," *The Tampa Tribune-Times*, September 8, 1996, 10.

9) Thor Kamban Biberman,, "El Nino Spawns Weird Events; Seafood Businesses Suffering," *San Diego Daily Transcript*, February 27, 1998, http://www.sddt.com/newslibrary/weather.html.

10) Associated Press, "Storms hit Midwest," *St. Petersburg Times*, July 19, 1996, Section 2A.

11) Pacenti, John, The Associated Press, "Experts warn of warming's dire results," *The Tampa Tribune-Times*, June 21, 1996, 6.

12) Hagee, *Beginning of the End*, 98.

13) Le Comte, Douglas, "Around the World," *Weatherwise*, February/March 1997, 29.

14) Le Comte, Douglas, "A Wet and Stormy Year," *Weatherwise*, February/March 1997, 15.

15) Henson, Robert, "How Dry We Were...A short but intense drought ravaged the Southwest and southern Plains," *Weatherwise*, February/March 1997, 17-18.

16) Associated Press, "Thousands ordered from homes in flooded West," *St. Petersburg Times*, January 3, 1997, Section 1A.

17) "Midwest corn crop woes could help South Carolina," *PALLADIUM-ITEM*, June 17, 1996, Section A7.

18) New York Times Wires, "Drought strangles the Plains," *St. Petersburg Times*, May 20, 1996, Section 1A.

19) Staff and wire reports, "Bad crop year means trouble for more than farmers," *PALLADIUM-ITEM*, June 1996.

20) Church, J. R., "The Jews Come Home [-] Return From Exile," *Prophecy in the News*, July 1996, 27.

21) *Strong's Exhaustive Concordance of the Bible*, pg. 610, Hebrew Section pg. 38, #2416 then to pg. 39, #2421.

22) *The Revell Bible Dictionary*, Fleming H. Revell a division of Baker Book House Company, 1990; 380, under "fig".

23) Associated Press, "Shalom. Salaam. Peace...Excerpts from Clinton's remarks," *St. Petersburg Times*, September 14, 1993, Section 2A.

24) Associated Press, "Shalom. Salaam. Peace...Excerpts from Arafat's remarks," *St. Petersburg Times*, September 14, 1993, Section 2A.

25) Associated Press, "Shalom. Salaam. Peace...Excerpts from Rabin's remarks," *St. Petersburg Times*, September 14, 1993, Section 2A.

26) Evans, Michael D., *Save Jerusalem*, Urgent Update Section (Second to last page), Bedford Books, 1995.

27) Evans, *Save Jerusalem*, 8-9.

28) *Strong's Exhaustive Concordance of the Bible*, pg. 857, Greek Section pg. 17, #803.

29) *Strong's Exhaustive Concordance of the Bible*, pg. 857, Hebrew Section pg. 20, #983 (look under "safely").

30) *Strong's Exhaustive Concordance of the Bible*, pg. 946, Hebrew Section pg. 66, #4376.

Chapter 2

1) *The Revell Bible Dictionary*, 78, under "apostasy."
2) *Strong's Exhaustive Concordance of the Bible*, pg. 598, Greek Section pg. 41, #2722.
3) *Strong's Exhaustive Concordance of the Bible*, pg. 598, Greek Section pg. 41, #2722.
4) Baxter, Irvin, Jr., *Understanding the Endtime*, (Teacher's Manual), Endtime, Inc., 1995, 44.
5) Baxter, *Understanding the Endtime*, (Teacher's Manual), 51.

Chapter 3

1) *Strong's Exhaustive Concordance of the Bible*, pg. 369, Hebrew Section pg. 70, #4672.
2) *Strong's Exhaustive Concordance of the Bible*, pg. 364, Hebrew Section pg. 69, #4581.
3) Stearman, Gary, "A Biblical Bird Disappears From the Israeli Landscape," *Prophecy in the News*, July 1996, 13.
4) Fletcher, Elaine Ruth, "Rabin death laden with religious symbols, ironies," *St. Petersburg Times*, November 11, 1995.
5) *Strong's Exhaustive Concordance of the Bible*, pg. 999, Hebrew Section pg. 76, #5065.
6) *The Merriam-Webster Thesaurus*, Pocket Books, a division of Simon & Schuster, Inc., New York, August 1978, 176.
7) Guralnik, David B., *Webster's New World Dictionary of the American Language*, Warner Communications Company (published by arrangement with Simon & Schuster, Inc.), 1984, 613.
8) *The Merriam-Webster Thesaurus*, 35.
9) *The Merriam-Webster Thesaurus*, 580.
10) Dissentshik, Ido, "Why Yitzhak Rabin changed his mind," *St. Petersburg Times*, September 14, 1993, Section 12A.
11) Landrey, Wilbur G., Compiled from Times Wires, "Netanyahu headed for win...Peace process is dealt a blow [-] The Likud leader 'is deeply committed' to continuing the

147

peace process, a spokesman says," *St. Petersburg Times*, May 31, 1996, Section A.

12) "Likud at odds," *The Economist*, February 10, 1996, 44.

13) Landrey, Wilbur G., "In Mideast, more courage needed," *St. Petersburg Times*, January 27, 1995, Section 2A.

14) Halevi, Yossi Klein, "Bibi Netanyahu's new Likud...THE SAVIOR," *The New Republic*, June 21, 1993, 20.

15) Halevi, Yossi Klein, "Bibi Netanyahu's new Likud...THE SAVIOR," *The New Republic*, June 21, 1993, 19.

16) "Likud at odds," *The Economist*, February 10, 1996, 43.

17) Wallsten, Peter, "Rabin's death leaves many Jews uncertain," *St. Petersburg Times*, November 20, 1995, Section 2A.

18) Compiled from Times Wires, "'A Martyr for Peace'...Israelis wonder what ties now bind," *St. Petersburg Times*, November 7, 1995, Section 1A.

19) Compiled from Times Wires, "Dazed Israelis mourn Rabin and ask, 'why?'," *St. Petersburg Times*, November 6, 1995, Section 1A.

20) *The Revell Bible Dictionary*, 277, under "Daniel, Book of."

21) Holmes, Charles W., "Current peace effort unlikely to survive," *The Tampa Tribune-Times*, May 31, 1996, Section 12A.

22) Katz, Lee Michael, "Anxious world waits as a new leader emerges," *USA Today*, June 3, 1996, Section 2A.

23) Landrey, Wilber G., "From Jordan's king, a hopeful note," *St. Petersburg Times*, June 5, 1996, Section 2A.

24) A Prophetic Publication of Mike Evans Ministries, "Jerusalem Betrayed...The Tragedy Continues In The Battle For Jerusalem." *The Jerusalem Prophecy*, Volume 4, April 1997, 2.

25) Los Angeles Times, "Brash 'Bibi' honed political skills along American lines," *St. Petersburg Times*, May 31, 1996, Section 2A.

26) Jerusalem, "Likud at odds," *The Economist*, February 10, 1996, 43-44.

27) Jerusalem, "Likud at odds," *The Economist*, February 10, 1996, 44.

28) Los Angeles Times, "Brash 'Bibi' honed political skills along American lines," *St. Petersburg Times*, May 31, 1996, Section 2A.

29) Halevi, Yossi Klein, "Bibi Netanyahu's new Likud...THE SAVIOR," *The New Republic*, June 21, 1993, 20.

30) Associated Press, "Netanyahu pledges to support peace," *PALLADIUM-ITEM*, June 3, 1996, Section 9A.

31) *Strong's Exhaustive Concordance of the Bible*, pg. 765, Hebrew Section pg. 115, #7857.

32) Landrey, Wilbur G., "Israel to chart changed course," *St. Petersburg Times*, June 2, 1996, Section A.

33) "Israeli military vote to decide who becomes prime minister," *The Tampa Tribune-Times*, May 31, 1996.

34) Landrey, Wilbur G., "Netanyahu headed for win...Peace process is dealt a blow," *St. Petersburg Times*, May 31, 1996, Section A.

35) Compiled from Times Wires, "Netanyahu headed for win," *St. Petersburg Times*, May 31, 1996, Section 9A.

36) "Israeli military vote to decide who becomes prime minister," *The Tampa Tribune-Times*, May 31, 1996, Section 12A.

37) "Israeli military vote to decide who becomes prime minister," *The Tampa Tribune-Times*, May 31, 1996, Section 12A.

38) Landrey, Wilbur G., "Netanyahu headed for win...Peace process is dealt a blow," *St. Petersburg Times*, May 31,1996, Section A.

39) *Strong's Exhaustive Concordance of the Bible*, pg. 590, Hebrew Section pg. 36, #2266.

40) Associated Press, "Israel may deal on land," *St. Petersburg Times*, June 22, 1996, Section 2A.

41) Associated Press, "Israel's leader swallows words, meets with Arafat," *The Tampa Tribune-Times*, September 5, 1996, Section 8A.

42) Dallas Morning News, "Netanyahu, Arafat meet, pledge to negotiate issues," *St. Petersburg Times*, September 5, 1996, Section 2A.

43) Dallas Morning News, "Netanyahu denounced for Arafat

handshake," *St. Petersburg Times*, September 6, 1996, Section A.

44) Payton, Jack R., "The hard challenge of Hebron deal lies ahead," *St. Petersburg Times*, January 16, 1997, Section 2A.
45) Vrazo, Fawn, "Both sides wary over peace deal," *St. Petersburg Times*, January 16, 1997, Section 2A.
46) Payton, Jack, "Netanyahu: no charges, but trouble not over," *St. Petersburg Times*, April 21, 1997, Section A.
47) Compiled from Times Wires, "Police seek Netanyahu indictment," *St. Petersburg Times*, April 17, 1997, Section 1A.
48) Compiled from Times Wires, "Police seek Netanyahu indictment," *St. Petersburg Times*, April 17, 1997, Section 1A.
49) Associated Press, "Prosecutors cite insufficient evidence," *St. Petersburg Times*, April 21, 1997, Section 7A.
50) Payton, Jack, "Netanyahu: no charges, but trouble not over," *St. Petersburg Times*, April 21, 1997, Section A.
51) Associated Press, "Netanyahu political allies wavering," *St. Petersburg Times*, April 19, 1997, Section 11A.
52) Payton, Jack, "Netanyahu: no charges, but trouble not over," *St. Petersburg Times*, April 21, 1997, Section 7A.
53) *Strong's Exhaustive Concordance of the Bible*, pg. 818, Hebrew Section pg. 62, #4082.
54) Mordecai, Victor, *Is Fanatic Islam a Global Threat?*, Springfield, Missouri, May 1996, 11-12.
55) An Associated Press report, "Netanyahu has words of peace for Egypt," *The Tampa Tribune-Times*, July 19, 1996, Section 3A.
56) Los Angeles Times, "Israeli leader tells U.S.: Security first," *St. Petersburg Times*, June 26, 1996, Section A.
57) Compiled from Times Wires, "Israel wants to jump to top peace issues," *St. Petersburg Times*, October 8, 1996, Section 2A.
58) *Jack Van Impe Presents*, Benjamin Netanyahu's presentation of the government to the Knesset, June 18, 1996, "The Twenty-Seventh Government of Israel June 1996," September 1996.

59) Urshan, Nathaniel A., General Superintendent, "Stop Look and Listen," *Pentecostal Herald*, August 1996, 3.

60) Baxter, Irvin Jr., "Red Heifer born in Israel...Sign From Heaven?," *ENDTIME Magazine*, Volume 7, Number 3, May/June 1997, 9.

61) *The Revell Bible Dictionary*, 1048; under Zion.

62) Smith, Larry T., *The Godhead Bible Study*, 1982, 24.

63) *Strong's Exhaustive Concordance of the Bible*, pg. 189, Hebrew Section pg. 58, #3794.

64) *Strong's Exhaustive Concordance of the Bible*, pg. 842, Hebrew Section pg. 113, #7725.

65) *Strong's Exhaustive Concordance of the Bible*, pg. 364, Hebrew Section pg. 86, #5800.

66) Smith, Larry T., *Rightly Dividing the Word*, H.W. Mullican, 1979, 13.

Chapter 4

1) *Strong's Exhaustive Concordance of the Bible*, pg. 842, Hebrew Section pg. 113, #7725.

2) *Strong's Exhaustive Concordance of the Bible*, pg. 740, Hebrew Section pg. 96, #6486.

3) *The Revell Bible Dictionary*, 769; under "perdition."

4) *Strong's Exhaustive Concordance of the Bible*, pg. 598, Greek Section pg. 41, #2722.

5) *Strong's Exhaustive Concordance of the Bible*, pg. 598, Greek Section pg. 41, #2722.

6) *The Revell Bible Dictionary*, 15; under "abyss."

7) *Strong's Exhaustive Concordance of the Bible*, pg. 80, Greek Section pg. 10, #305 and #303.

8) *The American Heritage Dictionary*, Houghton Mifflin Company, Dell Publishing, a division of Bantam Double-day Dell Publishing Group, Inc., New York, 1983, 584.

9) *Strong's Exhaustive Concordance of the Bible*, pg. 138, Greek Section pg. 7, #12.

10) *The Revell Bible Dictionary*, 15, under "abyss."

11) Twentier *and* Willhoite, *Search for Truth*, 107.

12) *Strong's Exhaustive Concordance of the Bible*, pg. 685, Hebrew Section pg. 45, #2917 and #2916.

13) *Strong's Exhaustive Concordance of the Bible*, pg. 286, Hebrew Section pg. 90, #6083.

14) *Strong's Exhaustive Concordance of the Bible*, pg. 197, Hebrew Section pg. 41, #2635 then to #2636.

15) *Strong's Exhaustive Concordance of the Bible*, pg. 877, Hebrew Section pg. 37, #2344.

16) *The Revell Bible Dictionary*, 769, under "perdition."

17) *Saint Joseph Edition of the New American Bible*, Catholic Book Publishing Co. New York, 1986, pg. 62 of the New Testament.

18) *New American Bible*, pg. 62 of the New Testament.

19) *New American Bible, (Zechariah 11:13)*.

20) *New American Bible,* (Acts 1:18, 19).

21) *Strong's Exhaustive Concordance of the Bible*, pg. 97, Hebrew Section pg. 36, #2256 then to #2254.

22) *Strong's Exhaustive Concordance of the Bible*, pg. 518, Hebrew Section pg. 55, #3627.

23) New York Times & Cox News Service, "Israel, Palestinians achieve Hebron deal," *St. Petersburg Times*, January 15, 1997, Section A.

24) *Hermon and Sharon Bailey Show*, HS97-2-26, "Middle East News Update," Guest: Jimmy Deyoung.

25) *The Revell Bible Dictionary*, 1121; under "Hinnom."

26) *New American Bible*, (Jeremiah 19:11).

Chapter 5

1) Church, J. R., "The Jews Come Home [-] Return From Exile," *Prophecy in the News*, July 1996, 25.

2) Mordecai, *Is Fanatic Islam A Global Threat?*, 12.

3) Mordecai, *Is Fanatic Islam A Global Threat?*, 11-12.

4) Associated Press, "Clinton calls a Mid-east Summit," *St. Petersburg Times*, September 30, 1996, Section A.

5) *Strong's Exhaustive Concordance of the Bible*, pg. 352, Hebrew Section pg. 106, #7223 and #7221 then to #7218.

6) *Strong's Exhaustive Concordance of the Bible*, pg. 432, Hebrew Section pg. 119, #8181 then to #8175.

7) *Strong's Exhaustive Concordance of the Bible*, pg. 377, Hebrew Section pg. 9, #155 and pg. 8, #117.

8) *Strong's Exhaustive Concordance of the Bible*, pg. 310, Hebrew Section pg. 92, #6215 and #6213.
9) *Strong's Exhaustive Concordance of the Bible*, pg. 505, Hebrew Section pg. 99, #6718 then to pg. 98, #6679.
10) *Strong's Exhaustive Concordance of the Bible*, pg. 296, Hebrew Section pg. 8, #123.
11) *Strong's Exhaustive Concordance of the Bible*, pg. 432, Hebrew Section pg. 119, #8163.
12) *The Merriam-Webster Thesaurus*, 625.
13) *The Merriam-Webster Thesaurus*, 578.
14) *Strong's Exhaustive Concordance of the Bible*, pg. 102, Greek Section, pg. 36, #2342.
15) *The Merriam-Webster Thesaurus*, 57.
16) *Strong's Exhaustive Concordance of the Bible*, pg. 102, Greek Section pg. 36, #2342 then to #2339.
17) *Strong's Exhaustive Concordance of the Bible*, pg. 1084, Hebrew Section pg. 122, #8380 then to #8382.
18) The *Revell Bible Dictionary*, 536, under "Jacob."
19) Guralnik, *Webster's New World Dictionary of the American Language*, 601.
20) *Strong's Exhaustive Concordance of the Bible*, pg. 984, Hebrew Section pg. 73, #4820 and pg. 109, #7411.
21) *Strong's Exhaustive Concordance of the Bible*, pg. 796, Hebrew Section pg. 124, #8535.
22) A Cox News Service Report, "Netanyahu's swearing - in bumpy," *The Tampa Tribune-Times*, June 19, 1996, Nation/World pg. 5.
23) Dallas Morning News, "Netanyahu, Arafat meet, pledge to negotiate issues," *St. Petersburg Times*, September 5, 1996, Section 2A.
24) Will, George F., "Netanyahu sticks to his promise," *St. Petersburg Times*, June 24, 1996, Section 7A.
25) Baxter, Irvin, "Rabbi - Richman of the Temple Institute," *ENDTIME Magazine*, September/October 1993, pg. 25.
26) Payton, Jack R., "World troubles await no holiday," *St. Petersburg Times*, December 17, 1996, Section A.
27) *The Merriam-Webster Thesaurus*, 483.
28) *The Merriam-Webster Thesaurus*, 312.

29) *Strong's Exhaustive Concordance of the Bible*, pg. 945, Hebrew Section pg. 34, #2102.

30) *Strong's Exhaustive Concordance of the Bible*, pg. 801, Hebrew Section pg. 77, #5138 and pg. 34, #2102.

31) *Strong's Exhaustive Concordance of the Bible*, pg. 831, Hebrew Section pg. 8, #122 then to #119.

32) Landrey, Wilbur G., "In Mideast: France in, U.S. out," *St. Petersburg Times*, October 22, 1996, Section A.

33) *The Revell Bible Dictionary*, 693, under "Micah, Book of."

34) Compiled from Times Wires, "Arabs protest holy site digging," *St. Petersburg Times*, September 25, 1996, Section 2A.

35) "Netanyahu, Arafat Summit Planned," *St. Petersburg Times*, September 26, 1996, Section A.

36) *Strong's Exhaustive Concordance of the Bible*, pg. 1077, Hebrew Section pg. 101, #6869.

Chapter 6

1) *Strong's Exhaustive Concordance of the Bible*, pg. 1096 (from Gen. 27:3), Hebrew Section pg. 99, #6720.

2) Guralnik, *Webster's New World Dictionary of the American Language*, 481.

3) Baxter, Irvin, "Gershon Salomon Head of the Temple Mount Faithful in Jerusalem-Part II," *ENDTIME Magazine*, January/February 1995, 11, 13.

4) *Strong's Exhaustive Concordance of the Bible*, pg. 416, Hebrew Section pg. 40, #2530.

5) *Strong's Exhaustive Concordance of the Bible*, pg. 825, Hebrew Section pg. 19, #899.

6) Guralnik, *Webster's New World Dictionary of the American Language*, 453.

7) Guralnik, *Webster's New World Dictionary of the American Language*, 460.

8) *Strong's Exhaustive Concordance of the Bible*, pg. 935, Hebrew Section pg. 86, #5785 and #5783.

9) *Strong's Exhaustive Concordance of the Bible*, pg. 150, Hebrew Section pg. 105, #7136.

10) *Strong's Exhaustive Concordance of the Bible*, pg. 948,

Hebrew Section pg. 21, #1121.

Chapter 7
1) Chung, David, et al., "Melchizedek," (excerpt from: Woolridge, Judith), *Holman Bible Dictionary for Windows*, Version 1.0g, 1994, Parsons Technology Portions, Holman Bible Publisher.
2) *The Merriam-Webster Thesaurus*, 295 (*see Ascribe, pg. 39).
3) *Strong's Exhaustive Concordance of the Bible*, pg. 820, Greek Section pg. 60, #4286, then to pg. 62, #4388.
4) *Strong's Exhaustive Concordance of the Bible*, pg. 307, Greek Section pg. 73, #5179.
5) *The Merriam-Webster Thesaurus*, 13.
6) *Jack Van Impe Presents*, Benjamin Netanyahu's presentation of the government to the Knesset, June 18, 1996, "The Twenty-Seventh Government of Israel June 1996," September 1996.

Chapter 8
1) *The Revell Bible Dictionary*, 960; under "Tabernacle."
2) Associated Press, "Bedouin woman's price for a little bit of freedom: death," *St. Petersburg Times*, August 13, 1996, Section 2A.
3) Guralnik, *Webster's New World Dictionary of the American Language*, 465.
4) Guralnik, *Webster's New World Dictionary of the American Language*, 664.
5) *Strong's Exhaustive Concordance of the Bible*, pg. 666, Hebrew Section pg. 61, #4060.
6) *Strong's Exhaustive Concordance of the Bible*, pg. 809, Hebrew Section pg. 54, #3548.
7) Guralnik, *Webster's New World Dictionary of the American Language*, 636.
8) Guralnik, *Webster's New World Dictionary of the American Language*, 453.
9) Guralnik, *Webster's New World Dictionary of the American Language*, 460.
10) *Strong's Exhaustive Concordance of the Bible*, pg. 377,

Hebrew Section pg. 19, #899.

11) Guralnik, *Webster's New World Dictionary of the American Language*, 184.

12) *Strong's Exhaustive Concordance of the Bible*, pg. 278, Hebrew Section pg. 57, #3717.

13) *Strong's Exhaustive Concordance of the Bible*, pg. 230, Hebrew Section pg. 52, #3407 then to #3415 then to pg. 110, #7489 then to pg. 109, #7462.

14) Guralnik, *Webster's New World Dictionary of the American Language*, 246.

15) *Strong's Exhaustive Concordance of the Bible*, pg. 362, Hebrew Section pg. 95, #6440.

16) *Strong's Exhaustive Concordance of the Bible*, pg. 613, Hebrew Section pg. 60, #3924 then to pg. 59 #3883.

17) *Strong's Exhaustive Concordance of the Bible*, pg. 296, Hebrew Section pg. 120, #8193 and pg. 83 #5595.

18) *Strong's Exhaustive Concordance of the Bible*, pg. 762, Hebrew Section pg. 103, #7020 then to pg. 102, #6972 and pg. 103 #7019.

19) *Strong's Exhaustive Concordance of the Bible*, pg. 222, Hebrew Section pg. 37, #2279 then to pg. 36 #2266.

20) Guralnik, *Webster's New World Dictionary of the American Language*, 480.

21) Guralnik, *Webster's New World Dictionary of the American Language*, 477.

22) *Strong's Exhaustive Concordance of the Bible*, pg. 994, Hebrew Section pg. 105, #7165 then to #7164.

23) *Strong's Exhaustive Concordance of the Bible*, pg. 222, Hebrew Section pg. 36, #2266.

24) *Strong's Exhaustive Concordance of the Bible*, pg. 837, Hebrew Section pg. 84, #5629 then to #5628.

25) *Strong's Exhaustive Concordance of the Bible*, pg. 432, Hebrew Section pg. 42, #2677 then to #2673.

26) *Strong's Exhaustive Concordance of the Bible*, pg. 230, Hebrew Section pg. 52, #3407 then to #3415.

27) *Strong's Exhaustive Concordance of the Bible*, pg. 95, Hebrew Section pg. 10, #268.

28) Guralnik, *Webster's New World Dictionary of the American*

Language, 338.

29) *Strong's Exhaustive Concordance of the Bible*, pg. 992, Hebrew Section pg. 74, #4908.

30) *The American Heritage Dictionary*, Houghton Mifflin Company, 1983, 275.

31) *Strong's Exhaustive Concordance of the Bible*, pg. 228, Hebrew Section pg. 14, #520.

32) *The Merriam-Webster Thesaurus*, 499.

33) *The Merriam-Webster Thesaurus*, 251.

34) *Strong's Exhaustive Concordance of the Bible*, pg. 925, Hebrew Section pg. 98, #6654.

35) *Strong's Exhaustive Concordance of the Bible*, pg. 224, Hebrew Section pg. 56, #3680.

36) *Strong's Exhaustive Concordance of the Bible*, pg. 224, Hebrew Section pg. 66, #4372 then to pg. 56, #3680 then to pg. 57, #3780 and #3677 and #3678.

37) *Strong's Exhaustive Concordance of the Bible*, pg. 827, Hebrew Section pg. 11, #352.

38) *Strong's Exhaustive Concordance of the Bible*, pg. 935, Hebrew Section pg. 86, #5785.

39) *The Revell Bible Dictionary*, 121-122; under "badger skin."

40) *Strong's Exhaustive Concordance of the Bible*, pg. 934, Greek Section pg. 38, #2523 then to #2516 then to pg. 39, #2596.

41) *The Revell Bible Dictionary*, 977; under "throne."

42) *The Revell Bible Dictionary*, 600; under "judgement."

43) *Strong's Exhaustive Concordance of the Bible*, pg. 133, Hebrew Section pg. 105, #7175.

44) *Strong's Exhaustive Concordance of the Bible*, pg. 920, Hebrew Section pg. 115, #7848 then to #7850 and pg. 113, #7752.

45) *Strong's Exhaustive Concordance of the Bible*, pg. 1182, Hebrew Section pg. 90, #6086 then to #6095.

46) *Strong's Exhaustive Concordance of the Bible*, pg. 973, Hebrew Section pg. 89, #5975.

47) *Strong's Exhaustive Concordance of the Bible*, pg. 1003, Hebrew Section pg. 47, #3027.

48) Twentier and Willhoite, *Search for Truth*, 141.

49) Guralnik, *Webster's New World Dictionary of the American Language*, 534.

50) *Strong's Exhaustive Concordance of the Bible*, pg. 123, Hebrew Section pg. 65, #4295 then to pg. 86, #5786, #5785 and #5783.

51) *Strong's Exhaustive Concordance of the Bible*, pg. 464, Hebrew Section pg. 106, #7218.

52) Guralnik, *Webster's New World Dictionary of the American Language*, 537.

53) Guralnik, *Webster's New World Dictionary of the American Language*, 555.

54) Guralnik, *Webster's New World Dictionary of the American Language*, 555

55) *Strong's Exhaustive Concordance of the Bible*, pg. 848, Hebrew Section pg. 45, #2885.

56) *Strong's Exhaustive Concordance of the Bible*, pg. 661, Greek Section pg. 77, #5480 then to #5482 then to pg. 21, #1125.

57) *Strong's Exhaustive Concordance of the Bible*, pg. 707, Greek Section pg. 52, #3686.

58) *The Merriam-Webster Thesaurus*, 381.

59) Guralnik, *Webster's New World Dictionary of the American Language*, 143.

60) *Strong's Exhaustive Concordance of the Bible*, pg. 732, Greek Section pg. 15, #706 and pg. 8, #142.

61) Guralnik, *Webster's New World Dictionary of the American Language*, 499.

Chapter 9

1) Unger, Merill F., *The New Unger's Bible Dictionary*, pg. 134.

2) *The Revell Bible Dictionary*, 121; under "Babylon."

3) *The Revell Bible Dictionary*, 688; under "Mene, mene, tekel, parsin."

4) *Strong's Exhaustive Concordance of the Bible*, pg. 784, Hebrew Section pg. 96, #6537.

Chapter 10

1) *The Revell Bible Dictionary*, 906; under "seed."

2) Baxter, *Understanding Endtime*, 122-123.
3) *Strong's Exhaustive Concordance of the Bible*, pg. 897, Hebrew Section pg. 36, #2234 then to #2233.
4) Baxter, *Understanding Endtime*, 123.
5) Twentier and Willhoite, *Search for Truth*, 258.
6) Unger, Merill F., *The New Unger's Bible Dictionary*, pg. 1,089.
7) *Strong's Exhaustive Concordance of the Bible*, pg. 173, Greek Section pg. 18, #941 then to #939.
8) *Strong's Exhaustive Concordance of the Bible*, pg. 572, Greek Section pg. 18, #935 then to #939.

Chapter 11
1) *Strong's Exhaustive Concordance of the Bible*, pg. 214, Hebrew Section pg. 25, #1396.
2) The *Revell Bible Dictionary*, 256; under "covenant."
3) *Strong's Exhaustive Concordance of the Bible*, pg. 659, Hebrew Section pg. 106, #7227.
4) Stearman, Gary, "May 19, 1993: The Covenant of Jerusalem is Signed!," *ENDTIME Magazine*, September-October 1993, pg. 10-11.
5) Rev. Mendenhall, Wednesday night sermon, 1997, (Upper Room Apostolic Church).
6) *The Revell Bible Dictionary*, 605; under "kingdom."

Chapter 12
1) *The Revell Bible Dictionary*, 556; under "Jesus Christ."
2) Smith, Larry, *The Godhead Bible Study*, 19.

9 781585 001576